Book Marketing
for the
FIRST-TIME
AUTHOR

An Author Your Ambition Book

by M.K. Williams

First Printing, 2020

Second Edition, 2022

Third Edition, 2025

ISBN: 978-1-952084-40-9 (Paperback), 978-1-952084-41-6 (Hardcover)

Library of Congress Control Number: 2020900863

All content reflects our opinion at a given time and can change as time progresses. All information should be taken as an opinion and should not be misconstrued for professional or legal advice. The contents of this book are informational in nature and are not legal or tax advice, and the authors and publishers are not engaged in the provision of legal, tax, or any other advice.

Links included in this eBook might be affiliate links. If you purchase a product or service with the links that I provide I may receive a small commission. There is no additional charge to you, but it can help me continue to create and put out more content. Thank you for supporting my work so I can continue to provide you with helpful content!

Printed by MK Williams Publishing, LLC in the United States of America.

authoryourambition@gmail.com

www.authoryourambition.com

Cover Design by 100Covers

Works by M.K. Williams

Fiction

The Project Collusion Series

Nailbiters
Architects

The Feminina Series

The Infinite-Infinite
The Alpha-Nina

Other Fiction

Escaping Avila Chase
Enemies of Peace
Interview with a #Vanlifer

Non-Fiction

Self-Publishing for the First-Time Author
How to Write Your First Novel: A Guide for Aspiring Fiction Authors
Going Wide: Self-Publishing Your Books Outside The Amazon Ecosystem
Author Your Ambition: The Complete Self-Publishing Workbook for First-Time Authors

Contents

Dedication   1

Introduction   2

1. Cover Design   5

2. Marketing in and on the Book   16

3. Your Author Platform   23

4. Build your Reviews Early   39

5. Where the Readers are   49

6. Advertising   58

7. Continuous Marketing Efforts   69

8. Building a Readership   74

9. Conclusion   77

Bibliography   79

Resources   80

Author Bio   82

Dedication:
To all the aspiring authors who dream, plan, write, and work hard to make it a reality.

Introduction

My Story

I spent quite a bit of time worrying when my first self-published novel, *Nailbiters*, was released into the world. Not about practical things. No. My head was in the clouds. Because certainly, the book was going to catch steam and become a best-seller overnight. It was a riveting story with amazing twists. The kind that people love. I worried that instant success would pose a threat to my work-life balance. How could I still maintain my great day-job if I was flying off to New York to appear on the *Today Show* to talk about my meteoric rise? How could I make sure to get enough time with my husband if I was going to have it written into a contract that if the film rights were sold that I had to be on set to ensure continuity?

These were the things I was worried about. It's almost comical when I reflect on it. I had done my research and I knew the obstacles in front of me, and still, I worried about the most ludicrous things. None of those worries were founded. No viral hit. No big talk shows. No on-set time required.

I'm glad that I did dream big though. What author doesn't picture themselves realizing these success markers? But just writing a great story isn't enough. Authors have to craft entire worlds, write perfect dialog, and **they have to market their books**.

Your Story

This book was marketed to you. Some way, somehow, you heard about it from a friend, you saw it online, you clicked on an ad, or liked a social media post. You had to hear about this book and then decide to read it. Think about how you've discovered books in the past. They were all marketed to you. Each of those authors (or their support teams) had to find a way to get their book in front of you.

Not all authors will fit this description, but many that I know do: we're shy, introverts who prefer the characters in our heads to people in real life. We're not the pushy sales type. How are we supposed to take a life-long aversion to putting ourselves out there and start selling people on our book? The first step is to realize that your mindset needs to shift. Your book is no longer your precious book baby, it is no longer just your art and expression in printed word. It has tremendous value to your reader, whether it is informational or entertaining. You need to focus on what the book will provide the person who reads it.

Just like writing the book itself, this step won't be easy, but it is necessary. What works for me may not work for you. And good grief, if you have a strategy that works, please share it with me! All the authors that I know are still searching for the elusive winning formula. And this formula is different for each genre and sub-genre.

As I detail for you the things that will and won't matter, the things that have and haven't worked, my goal is for you to find something that will resonate with you. Over the years, my writing has evolved, as has my marketing strategy for my books. Yours will too. Feel free to come back to this book time and time again to refresh on some concepts that can help as your book catalog grows.

I will walk you through the same thought process that I use to make sure every element of the book is optimized to help it sell. I look at the exterior and interior of the book before I work on the marketing and advertising strategy; the layout of this book follows that method. We'll start with the essentials (which also happens to be the items that you have the most control over): cover design and book descriptions. Then we will create your digital author platform, generate early buzz around the book, and secure rave reviews. Our last stop will be paid advertising. It is last for several reasons; most importantly, because if you don't do the first items right, you won't likely see success with ads.

This framework will help you as you make your to-do lists and get your books out to avid readers who constantly demand "more!"

Happy marketing!

Chapter One

Cover Design

Y our first and most notable marketing asset is your book cover. This is the first element of your book marketing strategy. You may have heard about email lists or paid ads. Those are important too, and we will cover them later in this book. But the first thing anyone will see about your book, whether you are promoting it to your subscribers, your social media followers, or in an ad, is the cover.

Judging a Book by its Cover

People will absolutely judge your book by its cover. It's not just a beauty contest either; although, a beautiful cover will certainly help. Your audience is looking for certain visual cues about your book. Have you ever looked at the bestseller lists for a given genre online? Do you notice that they all seem to follow a template? The historical fiction books generally have a frame around them with people in period dress on the cover. The romance books all have the hunky guy with the perfect pecs – although many now favor illustrations of the couple, a more socially acceptable cover for reading in public. The science fiction books set in space all have a background of the stars on them.

This isn't people being lazy or copy-cats. The author and their designer know what their audience wants to see. If I am trying to promote a sweet romance,

I'm not going to have the font on the cover look like it's written in blood. For a horror book, absolutely!

And the judging doesn't stop at the genre either. Certain colors or styles come and go into favor. You want your book to be on-trend, but not too late to the game. You want it to stand out so the reader will recognize it, but you don't want it to be so different that it doesn't match the readers' expectations. A review of the best books in your genre for several years will allow you to start to spot these trends. Some years solid bold colors were very big on cover design, but using them now may give your book a dated appearance. It is a fine balancing act.

As the production value of self-published books has improved, so has the quality of the cover design. There are still instances where you can look at the cover of a book and think instantly: "self-published." Likely because the author was trying to save money or try out their design skills, so they made the cover themselves. In most cases, a reader who isn't immersed in the minutiae of publishing won't be able to distinguish a self-published book from a traditionally published book just based on the cover alone. And that is a very good thing.

Most readers don't care how the book was published, they just want to be entertained and feel they got their money's worth. A solid cover design will help grab their attention.

Keep in mind that a reader may need to see the cover of your book several times before they decide to purchase it. The wow factor is important. Scroll through your genre on Goodreads, Amazon, or Barnes & Noble to get a feel for what the cover trends are. You can also look through Pinterest. My go-to is #bookstagram on Instagram. There are so many great accounts that feature beautiful photos of books. This gives me an idea of what looks good, what people like, and some creative ideas for how to stage photos for my own books. (I'll discuss each of these sites and online communities in more detail later in the book.)

No matter your book format, there will be a front cover visible. That's why it is the most important marketing element for your book. The cover image will be on any ads or marketing photos; it is a calling card for your book.

Spine Design

The design considerations don't stop at the front cover. The spine and back cover need to look appealing too. Think about the books that may be on your bookshelf right now. How many are facing out with the front cover on display? Probably none. If your book is in a bookstore or a library, it will be stacked in a row with the rest of the books and have the spine facing out. You need to make sure that your spine is just as appealing as the front. The title and your name should be clear with proper font sizing. There should be some element from the front or back cover that wraps around. This will catch the attention of a reader and get them to pick your book off the shelves.

To have any text on your spine, your printed book needs to have at least 70-100 pages. Aim for 100 pages as a minimum so that any text is legible. Most fiction books are much longer than this. For non-fiction, you may feel that 100 pages is enough to cover your topic. Just keep in mind the spine dimensions and design as you focus on your page length.

The spine doesn't matter for digital books. But if you are releasing your book in multiple formats, you will need to pay attention to this detail.

So now the question remains, who is going to make this beautiful, eye-catching design that will fit your genre but stand out?

Professional Design

Hiring an Artist

I have worked with professional artists and I have designed some of my own covers. Because of this experience, I can give you some perspective on both options.

My first recommendation is to work with a professional. This will add to your up-front costs. However, you already have a lot to manage and take care of. Hiring a professional allows you to focus on the other equally important factors when it comes to self-publishing your book. You also gain a specialized team member. Self-publishing can be a lonely process. A designer to help cheer on the success of the book will give you an extra boost of confidence as you get ready to launch. It will also give you peace of mind that your book is in the hands of a professional.

First, you need to think about what you want the cover to look like. Is it designed or illustrated or both? It took me a while to understand the distinction here, but it is important. An illustrator is someone who can hand-draw beautiful custom images. A designer is someone who uses graphic design software to put together images, shapes, and colors in a new way. Some designers are also illustrators. But not all designers are illustrators. If you have a vision for a hand-drawn image on your front cover, be sure to know that going in.

When looking to hire a designer, start within your network first. Do you know anyone who is a designer that has experience with book cover design? Ideally, you want to work with someone who knows books. If you know someone who has worked with a designer previously, you can ask for a reference. There is also a marketplace for independent publishers called Reedsy where you can search for cover designers, among other services.

Do some research before you hire someone. Do you like their other work? Keep in mind that the designer may have been asked to design something by another author that isn't your aesthetic; try to see as many samples as you can. The portfolio will help you to judge the quality of their work across multiple projects.

If you know someone who is an artist but hasn't necessarily worked on book covers before, that doesn't disqualify them. If you like their work and their aesthetic, this could still be a good fit. Ask them if they would be up to a new challenge and send them the cover requirements for the platforms that you plan to publish on. (Each self-publishing platform has easy to find style guides.) Design has its own specific language. If they are fluent, then they should be able to see exactly what you need in terms of dimension, color, and bleed/trim sizes.

As you negotiate the rate, you should keep their experience level in mind. Someone who has created many book covers knows their worth. Someone who is a talented artist looking to move into the book cover space still knows their worth. Be upfront about what you have budgeted and what you can afford.

I have worked with artists who charged $1,000 for the full interior formatting and cover design of a book. I have worked with others who charged $1,000 for just the cover design. A custom-designed piece that you will own is an investment. You may be able to negotiate a payment plan or royalty payment deal depending on the designer and your budget. Some designers may charge you much less (in the $300-$500 range), but be sure to vet them too. Don't just sign on with the least expensive person without first getting a feel for how they will communicate with you, what the final deliverables will be, and the schedule for your design and revision rounds. Even if you find a designer who will give you a cover for $100, if they don't communicate, are late on responding, or don't meet your needs, it is still $100 too much.

Book Cover Design Companies

If no one in your direct network is an artist or can recommend an artist, then it's time to search outside your network.

Many companies have formed that just focus on book cover design. Each company has a distinct pricing model and offers different packages. Some have preset designs you can scroll through. Usually, you can sort by genre. Since the design has already been set, you will purchase the design, send in your name and the book title, and receive that cover with your information filled in. In this model, you pay one rate to use the cover image on your book and a second rate to ensure that no one else can use it. These companies usually don't allow for revisions to the design: what you see is what you get. Some will allow for small modifications. Read the fine print before you pay.

Other sites allow you to put in the genre, title, and your name. Then they provide you with many designs to choose from, all without any revisions or editing rounds. 99Designs is a popular service for this type of design work.

One of the best sites I have found for self-publishing authors is 100Covers. They study book covers and stay on top of the latest trends in best-selling categories. While they have been around for many years, they have kept their prices low to help self-publishing authors get a great quality cover that won't blow their budget. They provide interior formatting now too!

Still another option to get a custom cover design that you know will not be used anywhere else would be to look on Fiverr or other similar websites. Usually, the design costs start at one price, but you can add on more to get additional options like a 3D mock-up.

There are a lot of options out there, and that can feel overwhelming. It's almost too many. But the great thing is that there is a designer out there who fits your unique needs and your budget. You get to find what works best for you.

Design Considerations

No matter who you hire, here are some things to keep in mind:

1. **Create a Pinterest mood board:** Start this during the drafting phase of your book. You can create private boards to keep track of covers that you like, design concepts that caught your eye, and even book covers that you don't like. You will start to notice a pattern with your pins. When you are working directly with a designer, this mood-board can help them get an idea of what you want. This can also help you understand if you need an illustrator. If all the designs you select are illustrations, then this will help you to narrow your search to someone who can do illustrations and cover design.

2. **Set your budget:** I have worked with designers who have charged up to $5,000 for a full interior formatting with 50+ illustrations and exterior book design. I have also worked with companies that charged $300 for a full print cover and a 3D mock-up. The prices can vary greatly based on the experience of the designer, the extent of the work to be done, and your budget. If you hire the best book designer in the world who has designed the cover of dozens of best-selling books, you will pay more for their experience. If you work with someone new to

book cover design, you should pay less. *Be realistic about what you can spend and be clear on what you will receive for your money.*

3. **What you should get**: When the work is done, you should have your eBook cover design, a full print cover (front, back, and spine), and a 3D mock-up. If you plan to do an audiobook now or in the future, ask for that format as well. You may also receive the working files. Most designers who have done book covers before, know to include each of these things. Someone new may not know to include this, so you should ask. Keep in mind that some companies that sell book covers just sell eBook covers, not full print covers or 3D mock-ups. Read the fine print. To get the working files you may have to pay more. Ask questions of the designer before you send in your payment.

4. **Edits and Revisions**: As writers, we are good with words, mostly. Every designer I have worked with has planned for at least 2 rounds of edits and revisions on design concepts. Your initial idea may sound great, but the execution may not be just right. The designer may have captured 90% of what you wanted the first time, but it may still need a little work. You want to be able to ask for something to be tweaked. This is your book baby after all and you need to feel confident in how it looks. But, on the other side of that coin, you need to be decisive. A professional designer has heard and received critical feedback from clients before. It is okay for you to say that you do not like a certain concept, but you need to say why. Is it the color scheme, is it the imagery? You need to explain what you do and do not like to help them as they make their edits. Help them get it right the next time.

One item that I mentioned above is very important, and that is access to the working files. When possible, I believe that you should own the working files for your book cover. This is one reason why I don't prefer to work with *some* book cover design companies. If they can resell the same design elsewhere, or if they upcharge you for the working files, it may not be obvious right away that you purchased a one-time product that you cannot change.

In my opinion, if you have paid for the artwork, you should be able to make any edits. At this point, you have hired a professional because you aren't going to be able to do the design work. But what if you need to change the back cover of your print book?

This was the exact situation I found myself in when a client needed a change made to their back cover. We had received several advance reviews back from big-names in our genre. These were the perfect quotes to put on the back of the book. I reached out to our original designer and asked if she could make the text changes for the paperback and hardback dust cover. I fully expected to have to pay for this change request, but I first needed to confirm that she had the time to make this change. A week went by and I didn't hear anything. We were close to the print deadline. We could have missed our opportunity to add these quotes. This would not have been the end of the world, but it would not have been ideal. Another designer who worked for this client on their web design said that she could make the text edits. Because we had the working files, we were able to make the edit and update the covers. I did hear back from our original designer a week later. She had been knocked out by a nasty flu and had only started to catch up on emails. I explained that we had another designer make the text edits to which she replied with great relief. If we had been beholden to her to make every little edit, and if all of her previous clients were beholden, her backlog of work from that cold would have been insane. The ability to access your working files will save you headaches and potentially expensive redesigns in the future.

Some designers can be very wary about sending over the working files. Perhaps a past client botched edits and then the work went out looking bad with the designer's name on it. Yikes. I find if you can explain *why* you want the working files (ability to make small edits just in case), but that you would be happy to work with them in the future for edits as well, it can alleviate the concern.

Designing Your Own Cover

Just as I have worked with professional designers, I have also designed my own book covers. You may select this option because you have a $0 budget for design, that is okay. Because you are new to self-publishing, you may only want to invest what you have earned into your books. You can always go back later and re-release the book with a new cover. While it is best to launch with your best foot forward, limited funds are a legitimate reason to design your cover.

If you have design skills, you can also elect to go this route. I know several authors who are multitalented and have amazing artistic skills they want to showcase. You may have the ability to do the design, but you still need to research book covers in your genre.

I designed the covers for several of my books because I like to learn. I have access to Adobe Photoshop and took a design course through Coursera (a free online course aggregator). Because I was new to this process, I had to remember to be patient. The original concept in my mind was very elaborate. I had to rethink and retool the cover based on my skill set.

I also make sure the images I use on the covers are ones that I own or have permission to use. This is a common mistake that first-time authors make when they design their own covers. There are free online tools that offer "book cover templates." However, the images and visual elements are not licensed for you to use on a money-making endeavor unless you upgrade to their paid subscription. Be careful of this.

Canva is an online design service that anyone can use to make beautiful book covers. Just be sure that you use images and graphics that you own or that you have paid for their upgraded features (still less expensive than a professional book cover designer) so that you can use those elements.

A word of caution on designing your book cover on Canva. At least once every weekend, I get a panicked message from a new author. Their cover has been rejected by KDP or IngramSpark. I advise them to use the cover templates either service provides. Then they ask me how to make that work in Canva. I'm sure there is an elaborate way, but this service seems best for making eBook covers instead of print covers that will be accepted by self-publishing platforms. Keep this in mind when you start designing.

Just as you would when you work with a professional designer, create a mood board on Pinterest. This can help you start to look at each design and figure out the elements and layers. How would you try to construct something similar? How could you practice the design skills necessary to create your vision?

Be sure to save all of your working files. If you run out of patience and decide to hire a designer down the line, it can be helpful to provide a designer with what you have already started. Or if you like the design, but you experience issues when you export the file, a professional may be able to help salvage what you have created.

To design your own cover, I would recommend you use Adobe Photoshop. Not only is it a very powerful tool, but there are many free tutorials available online. You can find these tutorials through Adobe or experienced designers on YouTube. They can show you exactly how to create a certain look or element. You can absolutely learn this software; it is just a matter of time and patience.

When you go to upload your cover design, be sure to evaluate the requirements carefully for each platform. Confirm the requirements and make note of which files can be used for multiple uploads and which can only be used for one platform. Save the file name to include the book title, platform, and dimensions so you can easily tell which file goes to a given platform. Some self-publishing platforms have different requirements for the color format (RGB v CMYK), how the color shows up (print quality, ICC profiles included or excluded), and sizing requirements (trim and bleed as well as file size).

Using A.I. To Create Book Covers

Since the first (and second) edition of this guide was published, there has been a boom in Artificial Intelligence (A.I.). While I would love to see this technology used to cure chronic illness and eliminate hunger, people seem to use it to create images and books instead. Alas.

At the time of this publication, many authors are making use of A.I. tools such as Midjourney or Dall-E to create character images, book promotions, and even cover art. While this is not illegal, many artists are concerned that their artwork was used without permission to train these programs. Which, from their point-of-view, is theft. Several court cases are pending that will *hopefully* allow for artists to be paid for their work to be used in training A.I. programs.

When it comes to cover art, there is nothing stopping an author from using an A.I. created cover at this time. Some readers are very against A.I. and may not purchase a book with an A.I. cover. Some may not notice or care.

When uploading to self-publishing platforms, you may be asked to disclose if the book - the interior or cover - was created with any A.I. assistance. Be honest here. If you are hiring someone to design a cover for you, ask them if they have used A.I. You need to be able to answer the question when you upload your book.

At this time, it appears to be a means to tally how frequently A.I. is used. My guess is that the platforms may invest in updating their cover-creators to use A.I. based on the popularity with authors.

Regardless of who designed the cover art, you or a hired professional, you need to give credit on your copyright page. When I work with a designer, I ask them to confirm how they would like their information displayed. When I create my own covers, I add a photo credit to the service where I purchased the stock photo for the background. Just as you would give proper credit to any sources in a bibliography, you should also give credit to the designer. This acts as a business card for the designer and adds legitimacy to your book as well.

As a thank-you to each designer, they have each received a copy of the finished paperback when the book is done. This is a nice way to close out the project and say thank you!

Now that your book has a face, let's move to the next most visible and important aspect in marketing your book: the book itself.

Chapter Two

Marketing in and on the Book

When you market your books, your competition isn't just other books on the market. It's every television show available on-demand through streaming services, instant access to social media feeds, and sleep.

If a reader has picked your book out of all the options available to them, you want to make sure they have a great experience. (You already did this when you wrote a great book.) Then you want them to return for more when your next book is released.

Who are your favorite authors whose books you anxiously await? That's the kind of energy you want to cultivate and that all starts when they read the first page.

Front Matter - Other Books

Okay, so the actual first page is your title page, and then your copyright page, but the *third* page is your list of other works. When I read a book by an author and I am blown away, I will flip to that list of "Other Works By..." and start to add a few to my Goodreads list. (We'll talk more about Goodreads later in Chapter 5.)

Once you have published several books, you can add this list as well. I didn't start to add this to my print and eBooks until my third book came out. Primarily because I thought it looked silly to have "Other Works by M.K. Williams" with only one book listed. Now, I break down my books by series, genre, and whether it is fiction or non-fiction. As my backlist grows, I will continue to adapt this list.

You can list the books in whatever order you see fit, but there should be a clear organization to the list. Some methods you can use for listing the books are:

- Chronologically based on their release date

- Alphabetically

- Group series together with non-series books on their own

- Group genres together: Fiction Works, Non-Fiction Works, Poetry, etc.

You can glance back at the front matter for this book to see how I have set mine as an example. Most people skip this, but as an author, I suggest that you take a look each time you open a book. You may be inspired to try a new method for how you list your books. And you may see that, yes, you can write non-fiction for personal finance and poetry because: you do you!

Back Matter - First Chapter of the Next Book

If you have written a real page-turner, people will want more. You can give them the first chapter of your next book to pique their interest and get them hooked on the next part of the story. This is especially true if your book is part of a series. I have always appreciated this when I have seen it in books that I enjoyed.

One logical strategy for your books is to include the first chapter of the next book in the series at the end of the first book. Great idea! Get 'em hooked. But if this is your first book, then you don't have the next chapter...yet.

I had a four-year gap between the first book in the Project Collusion Series (*Nailbiters*) and the second (*Architects*). The text for the first portion of book two was not written, edited, or finalized for quite some time. I couldn't add that content until the second book was done. Some authors who use the rapid-release method will already have this content done by the time Book 1 is ready for upload.

This is a long-term strategy to keep in your back pocket. As a self-published author, you have ultimate control over when you modify your manuscript. You can change the files for eBooks and Print at will (and mostly at no-cost, based on which platform you select). This is an advantage to using a self-publishing platform that does not charge you for edits or revisions.

As I started the manuscript for the sequel, I created a new project in Asana (a free online project management tool). After "write first draft" and "edit first draft," I listed "update *Nailbiters*" next. As an author, there are a lot of fine details to manage, and this is yet another one.

Some authors may suggest that you add a few sentences to offer the reader a chance to read the first chapter of the next book if they subscribe to your email list. I think this might annoy readers, but that is just me.

You should add that chapter once it is ready for print. At the end, let the reader know that they can learn more about the sequel and other books in the series if they subscribe. This way you have already given them something to keep them interested in the next book, and you offer them valuable information in exchange for their email address. Don't hold content hostage when you have a reader on the hook!

Back Matter - Thank You and Subscribe

If you read that last section and thought "uh, I have no intention to write a series," then no worries! You can still give the reader a little something more.

I always include a few sentences at the end of the book to thank the reader for taking the time to read the story. They could have been doing anything else, but they chose to read my book.

"Thank you for taking the time to read, TITLE. I hope that you
enjoyed reading this story as much as I enjoyed writing it."

I then make a simple appeal for an honest book review. I always make sure to explain the benefit to others. I'm not asking for myself. (Although, I clearly wouldn't say no to a windfall of 5-star reviews.) I am asking the reader to help the next person down the line. I am appealing to their altruistic nature.

"If you enjoyed this story, please take the time to leave a review.
This helps other readers discover this book."

Then you will want to close with an appeal to subscribe. You should know that I resisted this for YEARS. My previous day job involved email marketing. The last thing I wanted to do when I got home was to spend my precious writing hours doing more email marketing. But your email list is incredibly valuable as an author. These are the people who want to hear from you when you have a new book out or more information on your topic. In the past my appeal has been very simple; as you start out you may be more comfortable with this approach:

"For more information on current and forthcoming titles, you can
subscribe at 1MKWilliams.com"

This was my go-to. For several years, I heard other authors mention that they had earned subscribers with a "lead magnet" in their books. This is an industry term for an item that attracts users to complete a subscription form. I wrote fiction, and I had no idea what else I could offer readers to get them to subscribe. I have only now, several years in, started to add side-stories as my lead magnet. If you have some deleted pieces of the story or character content that you cut, this may be the kind of extra that your audience wants. Another option could be an alternative ending that you considered. But make sure that this side-story or additional content is just as well edited as the rest of the book.

If you wrote a non-fiction book, this tends to be a bit easier to figure out. What additional worksheet or content would your reader want or need after reading your book? That is your lead magnet. If you want to see an example, you can skip ahead to the end of this book.

> *"To access your FREE LEAD MAGNET NAME, visit author yourambition.com/LEADMAGNETNAME."*

The good news is that you can continue to evolve this over time and even test which language works best in your eBooks. You can go with one set of text when you launch the book and optimize it a month later to see if you notice a difference in how many email signups you receive. Once you have found the best text in your eBook, you can update your print books as well.

Book Description

Unless you have editorial quotes from a dozen reputable newspapers and acclaimed authors, you will likely put your book description on the back of your book. This copy will also go on your book's page on any retailers and review platforms. This description can be a chapter-by-chapter bullet point outline of what the reader will learn if you are writing non-fiction. For fiction, it can be a short and mysterious paragraph that will leave the reader wanting more.

After you have caught the eye of the reader with your cover, they will read your book description to see if this is something that they want to pick up. Spend some time looking at the descriptions of books in your genre. Do they start with a one-sentence headline or hook? Do they list out the action items from the how-to book? Are there only four lines on the plot and the rest of the description compares the book to others in the genre?

Use these other descriptions as research and craft several versions of your own. Always have someone else read or proof your description. This can be your editor or a friend. Nothing is more embarrassing than when you put all your effort into the book to then have someone comment that there is a typo in the first line of your book description. (Learned that one the hard way so you don't have to.) One tactic you can use is to craft a few options and let your friends select the one they would take action on. You may still have to optimize the text over time, but it will give you a solid place to start.

Book Description Exercise

Try to distill your book description down to one sentence, then one word. This one word should be the theme of your entire description. Here is an example from my first book, *Nailbiters*:

One Sentence Description: "Can Dora survive the invasion with her humanity intact?"

Drilling it Down: "Survive the invasion"

One Word: "Survive"

From there I can rebuild the description back up:

> *"Nailbiters* is a story of survival. On the morning of the invasion, Dora takes off running. She lasts three weeks before she is captured. Follow her story from the open plains of Texas to the desert of California. Readers have called this story "chilling" and "visceral." Find out why they haven't been able to put it down.

> Can Dora survive the invasion with her humanity intact? Read *Nailbiters* today to find out."

Try this exercise with your book. Revise and rework your description every few months. If you can't commit to that frequency, at least revisit it once a year. Each time you should start fresh, don't look at your current description.

You'll find that you have more to work with each time you revisit this important element to your book marketing strategy.

Now that you have a great cover and have each element within the book optimized, it is time to focus on the external elements that will be critical to your book's success: your author platform.

Chapter Three

Your Author Platform

To say that you have an "author platform" is a fancy way of putting your online presence as an author into one category. This is your website, your social media profiles, and all the channels that readers and other authors can connect with you and learn more about you and your books.

It would be nice if we could each write an amazing book and people would just know that it was high quality and purchase it. I would much rather write my next book than spend time optimizing my social channels. But these channels also give me a unique opportunity to connect. I can get direct feedback from readers who are excited their autographed copies of my books have just arrived. I can connect with other authors who have books on pre-order that I cannot wait to read. I can provide more background on who I am, and give new readers a chance to connect with me as a person and not just a name on a book cover.

Your platform is your voice in the book community. It is your business card, your home for all the information about your book, and the mountaintop you will shout the news of your book from.

But before you can holler "buy my book!" you have to build a foundation. You can't hit "publish" and then post about your book for the first time and expect amazing results. Are you building a social network of readers and fellow authors? Are you giving your followers behind-the-scenes pictures of your writing and editing process? As you start to build momentum for your book release, you want to continue a conversation with your fans, not just yell at them to buy your book. Show them some behind-the-scenes images of you at your writing space. Start to tell them that you are writing a book. Invite them to share their favorite authors or books.

You will have to tell them your book is on sale and you have to ask for their business. I have good friends who follow me on all of my author channels and still miss these announcements. Two weeks after I launched the presale of my fourth book, a friend commented on a post and congratulated me. But I made the announcement two weeks earlier. They had only just seen it on their feed. This happens because people are busy. People have other friends who post often and push down your content on their feed. People get busy and sometimes they don't go on social media. (I know, it's a crazy thought.)

This is where you have to find the right balance between genuine and promotional posts for your network. Below I will detail the elements that you can leverage to build your author platform.

Website

Of course, you need a website. This is your home online. You should include the information that is pertinent to who you are and the books that you write. Maybe you also offer an online course. Maybe you also have a desire to blog daily. All of this can live or link out from your website. It is your home; decorate it as you like. There will be several book-related platforms that will allow you to build a profile. But those will be uniform and limited. Your website is yours. You own it. You decide when it gets updated, what the visual theme is, etc.

When I first self-published my books, I was very intentional to only spend on items that I needed. I wanted my expenses to be as lean as possible so that I could recoup my costs and turn a profit. Even as I planned to operate on a slim budget and defer as many costs as I could, I still made sure to have a website with a ".com" domain. Not ".wordpress.com." Not ".wix.com." One that I owned.

When my first novel, *Nailbiters*, debuted, I also launched NailbitersNovel .com. Why not just "Nailbiters.com"? Well, it would have been very expensive and potentially misleading. I wanted people looking for the book on my website, not people with a bad habit.

After I published two more books, NailbitersNovel.com no longer made sense as the calling card for my author brand. I purchased 1MKWilliams.com and redirected every page on my website to this domain. This URL aligns with my social media accounts which are also @1MKWilliams. Look for a web domain that goes beyond just one book. A separate URL for each book can be easier for audiences to find. However, if you plan to write multiple books, you will either need to purchase and maintain a separate URL for each book (this can be costly in time and money), or you will want to create a catch-all URL. I wish I had just started with my name as my URL from the beginning, but this was a lesson learned.

I was able to purchase the domain via Wordpress.com and use their out-of-the-box templates. I may one day switch servers for added capabilities or optimize the design and hire that out to someone. But for now, this home that I have on the internet serves my needs. I would suggest that you invest in a ".com" domain name as well. If you believe that you will only ever write one book, then use the book title as the domain name. If you think that you will write multiple books, use your name as the domain. You could do both and hedge against someone else trying to purchase the domain later. The quantity of domains is really up to you and your budget, but have at least one place you can direct people to so that they can learn more about you.

And now that you have a website, what should go there?

Book Catalog

First and foremost, you should have information about your book on your author website. This should include the cover, your book description, and links to where the book can be purchased. From my experience, most of my book sales come from those who are already on retail websites or they have been told to seek out my book directly through a recommendation. But, for the small amount of traffic that goes to my website to learn more about my books, I want them to be able to easily click over to their preferred retailer and make that purchase.

As my catalog has expanded, I have revamped what each specific book page looks like, how I organize my website to categorize each book, and my menu layout. The point here is to make sure your book information is easy to find and up to date. Look at other authors in your genre for ideas and inspiration.

For books that I published several years ago, I have added reviews from different websites as well as links to articles about each book. If you know you have more than one book that you want to write, jot down the ideas that you have for how you will expand your website when the time comes.

Universal Book Links

Depending on your self-publishing strategy and which platforms you will upload your book to, you may have multiple retailers carrying your book. This is a good thing! But when you post about your book on social media or include it in a newsletter, which link should you use? Should you do individual posts on social media for each platform? Should you just tell people to go to Amazon and let them figure out how to find the book on other platforms?

Why make it more difficult for yourself and for your readers? With a Universal Book Link (UBL) you can have one page where your readers can easily find all the available links and then they can pick which vendor they prefer to purchase from. Draft2Digital is the self-publishing platform that furnishes these links via Books2Read. You don't have to self-publish via Draft2Digital to access these links.

I have set up Books2Read links for some of my books, but I only discovered this after I created similar pages on my own website. To me, it didn't make sense to have all my retailers on the book page on my website and a Books2Read UBL. If you don't currently have a website with all your retailers listed for your books, considered creating a UBL with Books2Read.

Biography

Your "About Me" page should tell your audience who you are and why they should care about your books. I start with a basic statement of how many books I have published, where I live, and which authors have influenced me.

Over time, I have added to this biography. When I looked at other author websites and those for creative entrepreneurs, I noticed they each had Press Kits. These were single webpages or PDFs that had all their highlights available in one place. As I started to branch out and try to schedule more interviews on podcasts, I found that it was convenient to have this Press Kit on my website with multiple versions of a biography, headshots, and links to previous interviews. This has helped me to easily find this information when I need to send it out, but it also adds legitimacy to my website and my marketing efforts.

- What should go in an extended biography on your website:

- The titles for each of your books

- Your academic credentials or experience in your topic (more important for non-fiction than fiction)

- Any awards or major accolades for your writing

- A "featured on" list

- Your passions outside of writing

Blog and Fresh Content

I have heard from bloggers and SEO (search engine optimization) experts that you need fresh content with lots of credible links to boost your search engine ranking. While I would love to be the top listing on Google or Bing for "what book should I read next?", I know that it would take a lot of time and effort to achieve. I'm not sure that would be the best use of my time.

While I know that SEO is vital to the success of my website, I would prefer if my books ranked higher on Amazon or Barnes & Noble to help with discoverability. I do occasionally add blog posts to my author website about books I am reading or using as research for my work-in-progress. But when it comes to writing, I would prefer to spend my time working on my next book, not blogging.

For first-time non-fiction authors, you may have arrived at your first book after years of blogging. If so, you already know how to produce fresh content regularly. If you are just starting as a non-fiction writer, you may find it isn't that hard to blog as you discover more about your topic and have more to share with your audience.

My solution for fresh content has been to automate my weekly instructional YouTube videos to post to my website blog. I generate weekly posts and further my mission to help aspiring authors with the information I put out. I see this as a win-win for me. It may be easy for you to maintain a blog on your topic. But for those of you reading this who aren't currently blogging, don't stress this too much as you get started. You may find that this is something you can add on as you develop more titles and want to tell your readers about your book development progress.

Subscribe

I've mentioned before that my day-job involved email marketing. I had to drive more email subscriptions for the companies that I worked for. I tested button colors to see which ones would grab someone's attention faster and had to constantly revise content to boost our conversion rates. I knew the value of growing an email list. Every self-publishing podcast I listened to (Kindlepreneur with Dave Chesson, The Creative Penn with Joanna Penn, and many others) stressed the importance of the email list. But with my limited free time, I just did not want to think about it.

This was a critical mistake. After three years, I had multiple books out and no real list to promote them to. Of course, I still used social media to market my books. As I continued to build my business, I focused more effort on growing my list of subscribers. Learn from my mistake, start this now.

But why should anyone subscribe to get emails from you? What value can you give them? If you wrote a non-fiction book, this answer is much easier. You can include planners and trackers; you can create worksheets or checklists all related to your topic. The list goes on.

For fiction, this can be a bit trickier. One thing I have done to grow my list of fiction subscribers is to offer side-stories. If someone enjoyed the book and wants to read more, they can subscribe. This is exactly the person who might also want to know when my next book in the series comes out.

Social Media

When I was a child and read my favorite books, I had no way to connect with the authors. I could send a postcard or letter, but a response was unlikely.

Now social media provides new and innovative ways to connect and follow your favorite authors. And that means there are many options for you to connect with your readers. Each author will find the right mix for them based on the platforms where they feel the most comfortable and which ones their readers make use of.

As a first-time author, you will have advice thrown at you from everyone and their brother about what you should or shouldn't do to market your book. Along with that will come information about all the different platforms that you can leverage to promote your books. The platforms I will review are the most popular. Some platforms become obsolete and new ones pop up. The main thing you need to remember is that each new platform you sign on for will take time away from writing your next book.

As Twitter (now X) has been abandoned by many authors, new platforms like Blue Sky or Mastodon have popped up. New entrants will continue to come and go. Experiment. Be strategic. Don't jump on to a new platform because "everyone else is." At a minimum, once you realize a new platform is here to stay, sign up for your account so no one can steal your preferred handle.

Below are some examples of channels that I have evaluated and what my decision was in terms of making use of them for my author platform.

Facebook

I set up a Facebook Business page for my Author Platform as soon as my first book launched. I invited my friends to follow it, some did, most didn't. In general, I try to keep my book posts on this page and not post them to my personal page at all. This is what works for me. You may want to share all of your book posts on your personal page. Do a test and figure out what works best for you.

After a few years of slow sales, I thought my Facebook Author's Page didn't contribute much to my platform. I didn't see many likes or comments on my posts. Then I looked at what other authors were doing. My posts at that time were very promotional. An image of the book cover and lots of text about "you can buy my book here." These posts looked rough. And they looked like ads. People don't go on Facebook to be sold to. They go there to connect with people, laugh at memes, and smile at pictures of dogs and cats.

In my very unscientific research, I noticed that most other authors or book-related pages posted photos of people out in the world and their book was strategically placed somewhere in the image. I started to do staged photoshoots with my books. On the sofa, in front of a fireplace, by the pool. Soon I started to get more engagement on my posts and readers actually started to send me photos of my books on their nightstands or at their local coffee houses.

You may soon realize that you have run out of creative ways to stage your book. Or perhaps the fan photos just haven't come in yet. I now use a service called BookBrush to create beautiful images that I can use on any social media platform. They have an excellent variety of mock-ups based on genre and you just upload your book cover and they blend it into the image naturally.

However you create the images you post, my suggestion is to treat your Facebook Author's Page as a place where you can connect with readers. Don't make every post promotional. Engage your followers in questions that will prompt responses.

After months of my new strategy of these lifestyle-focused images, I got busy. I was writing my fourth novel while working with two clients and still managing a full-time job. Something had to give. I pre-scheduled weekly posts on Facebook for a few months, but ultimately let that slip. It was more important to help my clients and get their books across the finish line.

And then my sales dipped. I figured this was because I had delayed the publication of my fourth book. I was focusing on my clients more than my own books.

One weekend I found myself with some extra time. My clients' manuscripts were with designers, and I had nothing that I could do for them at that moment. I found some additional photos and prescheduled some Facebook posts to re-engage my audience. The engagement wasn't overwhelming. But I did see a spike in book sales. While I have no direct connection between my Facebook posts and sales, I do know that when I don't post, I don't get sales. Maybe people aren't clicking through directly, but the book cover image is in their feed as a subtle reminder.

For me, I need to have this page and keep the feed fresh. It is a critical piece of a larger marketing puzzle. As you will find with your own platform, it is unlikely that just one element will be your silver bullet to success. It will be a combination and your overall presence that will be your biggest driver for book sales and reader engagement.

Instagram

Instagram is another great platform that you can leverage. But just like Facebook (its parent company), the algorithm tends to change often. Within the past year, I have found a great community of independent authors and writers on Instagram. They keep me motivated and inspired. I can also post updates on what I am writing and working on, but with a video via Instagram Stories.

For Instagram, you will need to decide if you want to maintain one account for all of your posts (both personal and book-related) or if you want to keep them separate. Some people keep their Instagram profiles private. But if you post about your book on a private channel, you may not get any notice outside of your immediate connections. In that case, you will want to have a separate account to promote your books. You will then need to build an audience for that new account. The decision is up to you, but if you decide to post about your books on your personal channel keep your genre audience in mind. If you write children's books, it may not be the best idea to post an Instagram story of you out at the bar with your friends.

One way that I have leveraged my personal connections via Instagram is to reach out to old college friends who now have large followings on the platform. Back in college, I couldn't have known they would become influencers; I was friends with them and we stayed connected via Facebook and Instagram over the years. One classmate started to share her elaborate nail art designs on social media after we graduated; she grew a large following. I always have chipped nails and would look at her artwork in awe. For my first book, *Nailbiters*, the cover art shows the main character biting at her nails. It was a bit of a stretch, but it was my first book and I tried every possible avenue I could think of. I reached out to see if she would create a series of nail designs based on the book. To my delight and surprise, she said yes and shared that she was a huge science-fiction fan. She devoured the book and put together three unique nail designs that she featured on her page. She needed new content and design ideas and I needed to get my book out to more people. It was a win-win.

Another friend was an interior design major who now makes a living painting watercolor designs for stationery and custom pieces for art collectors. Her work is amazing! With her background in interior design, she focused her channel on architectural scenes. When my third book, *Enemies of Peace*, was released, I reached out to see if she could do a design for my book. The story centered around a house and the setting became a character of its own. She did a beautiful painting of the house as I described it in the book and promoted it to her followers.

In both cases, my book was exposed to a totally new audience. While not everyone in those audiences likes to read or even enjoys my genre, it was great exposure. Also, it is always fun to support friends. The lesson here is to think outside the box and leverage your social connections where it can make sense.

TikTok (BookTok)

In the time since I first released this book, TikTok has exploded as a major social media platform. With that has come the subgenre known as BookTok. This is where avid readers and book influencers can make catchy short videos promoting books. It has been a new trend that many authors seem keen to jump on. If you are savvy with the app and enjoy working with short form video, this could be for you.

After delaying, I finally set up an account and began to post. It was hard work. The common advice I saw for authors was to post three times a day. THREE! Wow! While I know several authors who are crushing it on TikTok, the algorithm was crushing me. Or that's what it felt like. I challenged myself to post every day for a month. I made a study of what successful authors were doing: a mix of book reviews, acting as their characters, highlighted sections of the book, and some humorous author videos.

I did see, again, when I was consistent my book sales gradually increased. When I couldn't juggle drafting, editing, life, and posting – the daily posts were cut. My book sale declined.

If you are thinking about trying TikTok, remember to be authentic. If you hate the videos you are posting, people will be able to tell. Play to your strengths. Keep in mind that with any new platform and strategy there is a learning curve.

With each new channel, platform, or opportunity that comes along for you to market yourself and your book, you will need to decide how much time it will take to do it right and if you have the amount of effort to invest. Every minute you spend marketing is time away from writing your next book. You don't have to jump on each new trend. In fact, I suggest you err on the side of saying "no" to each new platform until you get to a "heck yes!" It will keep you from getting distracted and chasing shiny objects.

YouTube

I have a very real understanding of my creative limits. For a long time, I believed that I not only lacked the technical know-how and design vision to create videos, but I also had no equipment. Until I reached a point in 2018 when I realized that there was a very real threat to my limited writing time: answering questions from aspiring authors. I wanted to be the champion for others that I didn't have when I started my author journey. Many of the questions were the same, and I had a pre-made email ready to send when questions came in. But I always wanted to tinker with it to make it feel more personal. Ultimately, it took just as much time as if I didn't have a pre-written email ready to go.

I was stuck between helping others and enough writing time to finish my next book. Then I thought, if I could record my answers on video, they would seem more personal and still help others. And they could potentially help people who didn't even know me yet.

This is how my YouTube channel was born. It was a necessity, and it solved multiple problems. In the time that I have been creating videos, I have slowly improved my video and sound quality. I make no assertions that I am by any means an expert videographer. I aim to help others who want answers. (Which is also why I wrote this book because everyone learns and consumes information differently.)

It didn't make sense for me to start a YouTube channel when my first book was released. I added it to my author platform when it made sense. It has been a great tool to be able to connect with aspiring authors.

You will need to make the same assessment. If you are writing a non-fiction book, you may find that doing short informational videos on your topic can spread your message and increase book sales. If your book talks about health and wellness, maybe you will post stretching or exercise videos or guided meditations. If your book is intended to help people get out of debt, maybe you can feature videos where you interview people who have had success with your methods. If you are writing fiction, you may feature videos where you talk about the plot decisions that you made.

You can always add this to your Author Platform later. Before you start recording, be sure to make a list of potential videos. If you run out of ideas after five videos, you may be better off posting to your Facebook Author's page. Make sure you have enough ideas to keep you going for a while. YouTube rewards those who post consistently with better rankings in their algorithm.

To help authors get started with YouTube, I created the AuthorTube Premium Checklist. You can find it at AuthorYourAmbition.com/ultimate-chec klists/.

Pinterest

Pinterest, for all its expertly designed crafts and amazing recipes, is actually a search engine. When you go to your standard search engines like Google or Bing, you will see results pop up from Pinterest on the first page. Pinterest helps you to find and save things. While I have used Pinterest to create mood boards for cover art, I have not created a Pinterest channel for my author platform. The content on this platform is mostly visual and that is not my strength. I could make use of sites like Canva that offer templated designs. I could churn out great content and pin other related posts to my boards. I could do all of these things. But to do it right would take a lot of time away from all of the other things I need to be doing.

I have seen bloggers and podcasters successfully use this channel to drive more traffic to their websites. When they decided to write a book to support their brand, they were able to have a successful launch because of the regular traffic coming from Pinterest and other channels.

Just because this channel doesn't make sense for me right now, doesn't mean that it won't make sense for you. Does your book have a lot of visuals? Are you writing a non-fiction book that will reference planning guides, recipes, or other how-to instructional worksheets? Take a look at the other authors in your genre to see if they are using Pinterest and how they are making use of it. Then ask yourself if this is something you feel you must do to connect with readers or is this a nice-to-have for later?

Podcast(s)

Another way to build an audience and connect with them is through a podcast. You can launch a podcast easily and start uploading your ideas, interviews, and anything else you can think to put on a podcast. But you'll have to market that too. You'll need to find listeners who will subscribe and leave reviews. You'll have to pay some fees for hosting and maybe transcription too.

If you have a passion for your topic (and it aligns with your book content), a podcast can be an excellent extension of your brand and a great way to promote your book. I elected to not create a podcast. I have my YouTube channel where people can hear my thoughts, and I can keep my videos much shorter (5-8 minutes) than a typical podcast (30 minutes – 1 hour). For those who don't like to be in front of a camera, the podcast could be a great alternative.

If you are interested in starting a podcast to help build your author platform, I suggest reading *Podcasting for Authors: Creating Connections, Community, & Income* by Matty Dalrymple.

We will go over podcast guesting and being interviewed on podcasts in Chapter 7.

Posting Schedule

In the past, I used online services like Hootsuite to preschedule my content on social media. I would select the platform (Facebook, Twitter, or Instagram) and input the images and text. Once the post was scheduled I could duplicate it to post again later and drag and drop these items as the schedule needed to change.

Then they changed their plans and it would have been very pricey to stay on with that service. I didn't have a direct ROI to link back to social media. I wasn't about to spend more just on a scheduling service when I could invest that money elsewhere in my business.

I have settled on new a method for scheduling my social media posts. In Asana, I have a list of 90+ items I can talk about in relation to my books, my business, and my life. I set each topic on a 90-day rotation. Once it is complete, it will pop up again in three months. Some of these posts are promotional: purchase this book at Amazon, here is a 5-star review on Barnes & Noble, etc. Others are intentionally non-sales based. I have a list of my favorite podcasts, most anticipated new releases, and so much more.

I get a reminder in the morning to post and then I check it off for the day. I did all the work up front to craft the text and images for each post so I don't have to think about what I will post each day. It has already been decided.

Whichever task management software you make use of (Asana, Trello, Basecamp, Monday, etc.) they all work in the same way. You can create a calendar like this for yourself without having to pay for a scheduling service to navigate the tricky native scheduling systems on Facebook or Instagram.

Author Central

When I look back on my journey as an author, I am often amazed at how long it took me to find some of the most helpful items. It wasn't that I had blinders on to these helpful platforms; I just had so much to do for my day-job that marketing often took a back-seat. It was listening to the Kindlepreneur Podcast with Dave Chesson that I first heard about Author Central.

I was surprised that I hadn't heard about it earlier, especially because it is run by Amazon. That's right, the platform that I visit almost daily to check my sales numbers, also provides a powerful portal to see overall sales trends and rankings, opportunities to include editorial reviews, and the chance to curate a profile page to help me engage with readers on their website. I couldn't believe I had missed out on this platform.

I filled out my profile as soon as I learned about Author Central. I linked to my website so that new posts were shared automatically. I uploaded a book trailer and headshot. I made the most of this opportunity to get the right information in front of Amazon readers.

This is an important tool because it is likely that a large percentage of your sales will come from Amazon. If someone likes your book, they will (hopefully) go back and review it. If they really like it, they will click on your hyperlinked name just below the book title. When you don't have an author page set up, this link takes users to a results page as though the user had just searched for your name on the platform. When you have your Author Central profile set up, it takes them to your profile page with all of your books listed nicely for the reader to peruse and purchase.

One powerful element on this page is the "Follow" button. When a reader follows you, they will get an email from Amazon when you have a new book available for pre-order and when it releases. That is HUGE!

In terms of your author platform, having your Author Central page completed is a must-do item. You can also ensure that this is updated for international channels like amazon.co.uk., amazon.ca, amazon.mx, etc.

It is through Author Central that you will submit requests to update your book categories and other elements for your book as well. (NOTE: some troubleshooting you have to submit through KDP Helpdesk and some through Author Central. If you submit to the wrong one, they just tell you to submit to the other one.)

Now that we have a solid foundation for your digital presence as an author, we need to get your book out to the people. Next up, you need a street team and early reviews.

Chapter Four

Build your Reviews Early

To successfully launch your book, you are going to need some help. Among authors, those who help you out are called your street team. They will be the hype squad for your book. And they don't necessarily need to hit the streets posting flyers or spinning signs on the corner. They will repost all your tweets and 'grams about the book out to their network. They will cheer you on from the sidelines. And most importantly, they will leave honest reviews for your book. The reviews from your street team should be honest and fair.

Reviews are a big deal for any product sold anywhere on the internet, but they are crucial for books! When faced with an unlimited option of potential books, all of which will take time to read, your potential reader needs something to guide them. They need more than just your word that it is a good book. They want a detailed review of why a person did or did not like the book. They want to know why they should read it as well. As you gain more reviews, you get in front of more readers. Amazon and other online retailers can see when a product is selling well and highly rated. They only make money when your book sells so they can increase exposure for the products that have a high volume of 4- & 5-star reviews.

Some of your readers will love your book, some won't. The more people who like your books, the bigger your squad grows.

Beta Readers

I discussed beta readers in *Self-Publishing for the First-Time Author* as well. The purpose of this group is to read the manuscript before it is finished to give you feedback on the story and how it flows.

Because these are your earliest readers, they can also be the first fans of the book. Be sure to thank them for their help, keep them up to date on your progress, and let them know when the book releases. Since they read the book for no financial gain, they can provide an honest review of the book. (NOTE: if you have paid someone to be a beta reader, this does not apply.) After receiving feedback from your beta readers, you can probably tell who is going to give you a rave review and who might click on the 2-star option and give you a piece of their mind. While we all strive for the perfect 5-star rating, having an honest review from someone saying, "this book wasn't for me because..." can actually help you. A negative review that contains details of what that reader didn't enjoy may turn away other readers who might feel the same way. It also informs readers who may think, "well, those are all the things that I like."

Your beta readers have already done the time-intensive work of reading your book and providing feedback. You may find it easy at this point to ask them to share the news of your book on their networks. It is ridiculously easy for someone to click "share" or "retweet." After all, this group got an exclusive sneak peek of your book for free. This is their chance to brag about it to all of their friends while also promoting your book.

First Reviewers

Reviews are social proof that the book you have written is good. It passed another person's judgment and they deemed it worthy. Reviews also help other readers to discover your book. Have you ever noticed that after you have left a review or rating for any item online, that you will then see a page or ad pop up that says, "Users who enjoyed X also enjoyed Y"?

This works the same with books. If a reader reviews a book in your genre, gives it a 5-star rating, and then reads and reviews your book, also giving it a 5-star rating, the algorithm will learn that readers who liked the first book may also like the second. Reviews from "verified purchases" on the platform are usually weighted higher.

But getting those first reviews can be painful. For starters, when was the last time you reviewed a purchase that you made? Probably when something went horribly wrong. As an author, I take the time to at least rate every book I read and try to leave a review when I have a moment. Because I understand the importance of this for my own work, I want to make sure I do this for others.

Giving free review copies to your beta readers and others is one way to help generate those initial reviews. The reviewers should disclose that they received a free copy in exchange for an honest review. But, consider how many free review copies you are giving out and if that person is likely to leave a review.

In my early days, I was happy to send out as many free review copies as possible in the hopes of getting reviews. Only a fraction of people actually followed through. I've since narrowed my list and send roughly 8 to 12 free review copies out to those who I know will take action right away. (I have known others who gave away 50+ books based on their strategy and their list; you will need to evaluate this for yourself.) I keep a few copies in reserve for new potential reviewers as well. After your first book, you will see who is taking action and leaving that review. This will help you to narrow your list.

Another distinct method for generating reviews is to find ARC readers. ARC stands for Advance Reader Copy or Advance Review Copy. Effectively, these are free copies of your finished book you send out to readers for the express purpose of generating reviews. Because they are seeing a finished copy of the book that is ready to print, and not a manuscript in development, they are distinct from beta readers.

If you have connections to established people in your genre or big media names, you can send an ARC copy of your book to get an Editorial Review. As a new author, the best source for these reviews will be from other independent or self-published authors that you connect with. They understand the importance of those early reviews and are always looking for new books to read.

For those in your network who couldn't commit to the feedback requirement of being a beta reader, they may still be a great ARC reader. You can ask your list of email subscribers to join your ARC team as well. Be sure that these readers have joined a specific ARC list. Don't just send a free copy of your book to everyone on your email list. Be sure that whoever receives an ARC copy has indicated that they *want to read the book* and that *they will read it* by the time the book releases.

Book P.R. And Organized Social Media Book Tours

The marketing landscape for self-published books has changed so much since I first published *Nailbiters* a decade ago. I took a chance and worked with a company that hosted digital book tours. They organized a list of book bloggers who would all receive an early copy of the book as well as the cover art. Each reviewer posted a thoughtful blog about the book. Because they self-selected to read the book, these were all positive reviews. Within the first month of publication real world bloggers were buzzing about *Nailbiters*. I shared these posts as social proof that my book was worthy. But then, no new bloggers were reaching out. I didn't get the viral book moment I had been waiting for. I loved the exposure, but I didn't hire them again for another tour.

Fast forward to today, when Book P.R. is buzzing once again. In the interim, I've seen companies come and go that all promise authors a chance to get their books reviewed by bloggers and now bookstagrammers or booktokers. Some are legit, some are very questionable.

When I first heard of authors working with a P.R. team, I imagined that they contracted with a big Public Relations firm in New York City for upwards of five-figures. Not in my budget.

What these Book P.R. companies actually are is a much more organized version of the digital book tour I worked with a decade ago. Yes, some authors work with P.R. professionals to pitch their books to major news outlets. (That is the really expensive Manhattan P.R.) But, the majority of Book P.R. that you'll see advertised to you include a team of managers who maintain relationships with a broad list of book reviewers on social media. Authors will sign up for help launching their book. It can be marketing support for the entire launch with physical ARCs and swag being sent to reviewers, or helping to find and vet digital ARC readers. The size and quality of their list is key.

I was able to test a service last year to reinvigorate a book that had been out for two years. The company sent the details of my book to their list. Those interested signed on to receive a free copy in exchange for a review. Most reviewers posted on Goodreads, Amazon, as well as on their Instagram accounts. My effort was minimal and it had great results.

When engaging with a Book P.R. or Digital Book Tour company be clear about what they will do, what is expected of their reviewers, and what you need to provide. Also be clear on dates for when the ARC or Reviewer list will open, when the book will be distributed, and when they will be asked to post their review by.

When searching for a Book P.R. team to work with, ask other authors about their experience. You'll learn about what they did or didn't like and any specific items to look out for.

Some services specialize in specific genres or have de-facto specializations if the majority of reviewers on their list tend to prefer one genre. Ask what genres their list prefers. If you write science fiction and their list primarily reads romance, you may not get many interested readers, or you may get subpar reviews if your book just isn't a right fit for those readers.

These can be a great help in building an audience, curating a street team, or reaching out to a new audience. Always ask for the full price up front so you can evaluate if this service is within your budget.

Push Reviews Across Platforms

If you have 100 5-star reviews on Amazon (good for you!), but no ratings on Barnes & Noble, what do you think those B&N shoppers will do? They may keep scrolling past your book. Yes, Amazon holds the market share as of this publication. But it likely won't have that status forever. Start to encourage your readers to leave a review on the platform they purchased the book from.

When I noticed my sales increasing on platforms outside of the Amazon ecosystem, I made a point to promote that my books were on these platforms. As I optimize my marketing text for sales, I have also optimized my review reminders. I am still working to build these reviews organically on more retailers. This is a long and slow road, but I am in this for the long haul, so I don't mind rolling up my sleeves and doing the hard work.

One way I do this is that I ask for the review whenever someone tells me that they read my book and loved it, or that they are in the middle of the book and they are enjoying it. I follow this script (roughly):

Reader: Hey, M.K.! I'm reading BOOK TITLE right now, it's really good!

Me: I'm so glad you're enjoying the BOOK. When you finish reading, would you be willing to leave a review so other readers can find out what you liked about the book?

Reader: Sure/Yep/Okay

I feel awkward every time I ask, but this is an important step. Usually, I don't get an update from the reader. I just notice that I have another review one day. Sometimes I'll get a follow-up note from them saying that they left the review on Amazon or Goodreads or another platform. I make a point to promote 5-star reviews on my Author Facebook Page and Twitter to highlight the positive comments and (hopefully) encourage more.

Your First Negative Review

In early 2016, I hustled as much as I knew how to at that time to get *Nailbiters* in front of anyone that I could. Book bloggers, book reviewers, book enthusiasts.

Anyone who liked to read books was on my hit list. I scoured the Goodreads forums for book bloggers who were open to submissions. I stayed away from those who didn't like science fiction. *Nailbiters* is a sci-fi thriller, closer to sci-fi horror.

I connected with a book blogger on Goodreads who lived in the American Southwest, where *Nailbiters* was set. She wanted to do more author interviews on her blog, so we connected and did an interview. She asked if she could read *Nailbiters* as well to do a second post. I was excited, but I saw on her website that she listed romance and westerns as her preferred genres. I told her that Nailbiters was out of her normal reading preference, but she said she wanted to give it a try.

Well, no surprise, she didn't like it. She posted my interview and then a few weeks later posted a long review of my book and all the reasons she didn't like science fiction. She gave the book a 2-star rating on Goodreads and said: "not my cup of tea." NO DUH! This was an important lesson for me.

1. Not everyone will like your book, and that's okay because you don't like every book.

2. People know their genres, stop trying to change them.

3. Bad reviews are part of the process.

I was new to self-publishing. I had a handful of reviews and here was a big red 2-star review. I was crushed. I felt used. I wanted to write to her and ask her to take it down. But instead, I moved on. I focused on finding readers who liked sci-fi and asked them to read and review my book.

Your first negative review will sting. I've had more negative reviews since then, but I have had even more positive reviews. It's funny how a dozen positive reviews can feel like they mean nothing when you get a negative review. But you have to learn to laugh it off. I had another negative review for *Nailbiters* where the reader kept going on and on about how nothing in the plot had actually happened. *Nailbiters* is about an alien invasion **and it's fiction**. Of course, it never happened. I laughed this person off and wondered at how they didn't understand that this was a fictional tale.

Learn to either not look at your reviews or laugh off the bad ones. They're inevitable. Don't spend time and energy on the bad reviews when you could be writing your next book.

Ethics in Reviews

For as long as I have had books for sale, I have received emails from different services that promise to help me sell more books. The sender always asks if I would kindly pay them $100 (or more) for their review package.

The truth is that more reviews do help to sell more books. But reviews do not <u>guarantee</u> sales. Paid reviews are not only unethical, they can get you booted from Amazon or other retailers. There are paid services available to self-published and independent authors that promise an honest review (good or bad) after paying the submission fee. These services can be used as Editorial Reviews, but not as customer reviews. Editorial Reviews are perceived to be slightly better, but they will not impact your rankings.

Paid reviews are like paid friends; they're not genuine. The money you spent on that review could have gone into Facebook ads to promote your book, review copies mailed to influencers, or literally anything else to help move the needle on your business.

A year or so after I published my first books, Amazon had a real nasty situation on their hands. There was an influx of sellers on their website. Not just for books, for all kinds of items. Some sellers paid to get positive reviews on their goods. They also had sellers who paid people to write negative reviews on their competitors' pages. It was bad. Amazon has a lot of trust built with their consumer. If people can't trust the reviews, then how can they make the best decision on what to purchase? Amazon did a big crackdown on all reviews across the website. One morning I checked my Author Central page and saw that I had fewer reviews than the day before. As a new author with two books and less than 50 reviews between them, I was in a panic. I had toiled for those reviews, and now they were gone. I submitted a helpdesk ticket immediately and asked why they were removed. I was told that Amazon suspected these were paid reviews. I wrote back that I had never paid for a review and would never do that. I had worked hard to earn my reviews. I'm not sure if my emotional plea worked or whether someone on the back-end just cleared the reviews because they reappeared a few days later. Thank goodness.

What if Amazon hadn't believed me? They have banned sellers who violated the terms of service. This is about more than just paid reviews. For example, if you have a friend who says to you, "I want to support your book launch. But I don't have time to read it. Can you just tell me what to write in a review?" That's nice they want to help. However, if Amazon saw that interaction, their review would be blocked and your account would be flagged.

Another common practice I have seen authors do is exchange books and reviews. In concept this sounds nice: authors work together to help each other. But when you step back for a moment, you see that there are incentives here that aren't in the best interest of the prospective reader. If someone trades a book with me for a review, I may read the book, love it, and give them a great review. When they see that review, will it bias their own? What if they read my book and didn't like it? When they see my review, they may feel pressure to reciprocate. What if they post a 3-star review of my book before I finish reading their book? I may have been enjoying it, but I may feel slighted and post a less favorable review than I might have otherwise. In the end, book swaps pressure the authors to give each other the highest ratings possible. And Amazon can see if you trade reviews with another user on their platform. This will also be flagged. Even if you both genuinely enjoyed each other's book and left honest reviews, they could both be removed.

Amazon's review policy continues to evolve as they run into more users who try to work the system. I highly recommend that you read through it. If you ever think, "hmm, will this violate the review policy?" chances are that it will. But double-check just to be sure.

Amazon's Review Policy:

https://www.amazon.com/gp/help/customer/display.html?nodeId=201967050

By now, you know that your digital presence and early reviews are important. You can post promotions for your book and your hype squad will share them. You have advance reviews lined up for your book, and the interior and exterior are just right. With your beta readers, you found a small audience that you already know. But, what about the readers outside of your immediate network? Where are they, and how can you reach them? We'll discuss that next.

Chapter Five

Where the Readers are

I live near a major intersection. This can be convenient because there is a grocery store less than a mile from me. But it can be inconvenient too because of the congestion at the traffic light. I could try to take advantage of this prime location and stand outside with a large piece of cardboard that says "Ask Me About My Books." With the thousands of cars that pass by every day, I could get great exposure for my books. Right? WRONG!

As much as you believe that everyone who picks up your book will love it, they won't. Most people don't even like to read books. A Pew Research study released in 2019 reported that the average American reads 12 books a year. That is roughly one per month. But this is the mean. If you take out the book lovers and the complete non-readers, we are left with a median of only 4 books per year. That means most people won't read your book. This is why standing at a busy intersection would do nothing for my book sales.

You don't want to market your book to the masses at large. You want to market your book to readers. The people who read more than 12 books a year. The people who read every day on their commute to work and who join book clubs. You want your book to be where the readers are.

Thanks to the wonder of the internet: book nerds and bibliophiles can connect in so many different ways. This is great for you as an author and a reader!

Just as you researched the cover art for your genre, you will want to look at the other digital trends when it comes to marketing. If you wrote a self-help memoir, are the other authors in your space going on podcasts to promote their book? That is an indicator that you may want to do that as well. Did you write an epic space fantasy series? Maybe a visit to your local comic-con could expose you to the right audience for your book.

But, before you dive into these niche events or promotions, there are more basic steps to take first where you can easily get in front of avid readers.

Goodreads

I've mentioned this platform several times because there is no way to talk about marketing your book without mentioning Goodreads. They are certainly critical to my marketing mix. If I had to give up Facebook or Goodreads, I would stick with Goodreads. It's amazing! You can connect to your friends who love books, you can see new books that come out, and review the books that you've read. You can see stats on how many books you are reading. When you rate a book, it will update its algorithm to show you more of what you like. I go on "to be read" sprees and add books to my digital shelf at least once a month. If you love books, Goodreads can be a blessing and a curse because you can find so many books to read.

Whenever I talk to a friend or acquaintance who likes to discuss books, I usually come away with at least three books that I need to send to them. When I ask if they are on Goodreads and they say yes, I can recommend the book to them in one click. It's so easy. When they say that they aren't on Goodreads, I ask them how they can like books and not be on this platform. This is the perfect social platform for people who love books. **Book lovers are here.**

This means that as an author, you need to be there. You can claim a profile that will give you a little star icon to designate you as an author on the platform. You can fill out your biography and claim all of your titles so that they are linked to your profile. You can also list your favorite authors and influences. Readers can follow your profile for updates on your upcoming books. Through Goodreads, you can list the books you are currently reading on special digital shelves. I keep a list of books that I am reading as I research my next novel. This is a fun way to keep followers engaged in the process.

As readers add your books to their "Want to Read" or "Currently Reading" shelves you can see how many people want to read your book on your Author Dashboard. This is exciting, but don't check it too often. You can lose a lot of time if you focus on this metric instead of bigger marketing tasks or writing your next book.

You can also see when readers leave reviews about your book. I find that someone who regularly uses Goodreads is more likely to leave a review than a reader who peruses Amazon or other online retailers. Goodreads users are automatically prompted to leave a rating when they mark a book as "finished" and most people do. The reviews, even when they aren't a rave, are usually constructive and helpful to future readers.

Goodreads is an amazing tool for avid readers. As an author, you should maintain a presence on this platform to stay engaged with the people who are the most likely to read your books as you release more.

Where the Authors are

Because Goodreads is a great resource for readers, it is also a great resource for authors. Every great author is first a great reader. Many authors use the platform for their personal reading challenges and tracking. Within Goodreads, you can join groups of people who like the same books as you. There are also groups for authors, indie authors, self-published authors, authors with books that have just released, marketing best practices, etc.

I joined these groups when I first published and this was the perfect move. I connected with authors who were one step ahead of me. We learned from each other and shared in our small victories. I discovered the acronyms that now seem to be a second language. I connected with authors in other genres who are now good friends. I did an ARC Review for one author and now I am on her street team. I get to read each of her books when they come out – for free! Over the years, I haven't been able to spend as much time connecting and commenting. I still find that the author community on Goodreads is strong and supportive.

StoryGraph

A lot has changed since I first published this guide. Goodreads is now owned by Amazon, for better or worse. It has also had its fair share of issues with allowing users to rate books that haven't been published. Great for ARC readers to follow-through on leaving a review. Not great when the mob decides to 'cancel' a book based on diverse characters and inclusive story-lines.

StoryGraph is the biggest competitor to Goodreads. It is not owned by Amazon. It does allow people to review before a book has been published, but because it is a smaller community there appear to only be genuine readers on the platform. No trolls... yet.

The unique advantage to readers on this platform is the beautiful graphs and charts that track reading throughout the year. You can see your most read genre, your average ratings, how many pages you read a month. Wow! Data and book nerds unite!

StoryGraph doesn't offer a consolidated author dashboard. They do allow authors to market their books on the platform with giveaways, similar to Goodreads. As the network grows, I'd expect more features to help authors promote and connect will follow.

BookBub

When I shared with close friends that I planned to self-publish my first book, most were extremely supportive. One of my friends is always reading a new book series, so she was particularly excited for me. The first thing she said to me was, "you have to be on BookBub!" I had never heard of this site before, so I went to check it out. Similar to Goodreads, readers can sign up with a profile, select their favorite books, follow their favorite authors, and get emails about new releases.

One of the biggest benefits to readers who use this site is the daily deals emails that BookBub sends out featuring new releases and free books. Yes, free books! Because readers pay nothing to be part of this service, the value for them is incredible. If you love to read, you likely have to find a way to fund your habit. Free books are the answer for these voracious readers.

I'll discuss the Daily Deals more in the next chapter as we look into paid advertising, but you can still leverage this platform at no cost. To do this, set up an Author Profile on BookBub. You'll follow the same process as with Goodreads and input your biography, add a profile picture, and claim your books. As you create more accounts, the process will start to go faster.

This is another login to manage, so I suggest using a Password Manager to keep your logins secure. I also use a free project management software called Asana to keep track of what I need to do every time I release a book. Updating my BookBub (and other associated profiles) is on that list.

Let your followers know that you have a profile and encourage them to follow you here as well. In reality, some of your readers will follow you on Goodreads, others on BookBub, and still more will elect to follow you on other channels. The point here is that you should be on each platform to connect with your readers.

When you add a new book to your profile, BookBub will include your book in the newsletter they send to your followers. This is another touchpoint or reminder for them to read your book.

Bookstagram

Within the many Instagram sub-cultures is #BookStagram. Search for this hashtag and prepare to see your feed flooded with beautifully posed book images. There is an entire community of book lovers and book reviewers who post visually captivating photos of books. Some do this just because they love books. Others have parlayed their love of books into a business and receive free copies from publishers in exchange for a post on their channel. I would recommend following the accounts that cover books in your genre and whose aesthetic style appeals to you. I get ideas for my own book-related posts from these channels.

Try to build a genuine connection with any of these accounts before you reach out and ask them to review your book. Many of these influencers receive boxes and boxes of books from traditional publishers (some wanted, some unwanted). Their time is limited, build a relationship before you ask them to review your book.

Book Stores in Your Area

As you may have heard, retail is dying. Brick and mortar stores struggle to get people to come in and make a purchase on the spot. Many people will go into a store, find an item they like, and search for it on their smartphones while in the store to see if they can get a better deal from an online retailer. (This is called "showrooming.") You can't blame people who want a good deal. As online retailers continue to offer free shipping, why wouldn't someone order online unless they needed that item right away? It is important to understand what your local bookstore is up against before you approach them to ask for their help.

They need people who will come into the store and make a purchase. A book reading followed by a signing helps to drive sales for the store. The customer can't meet the author and get an autographed copy of the book online. They will purchase the experience when they buy your book at a local bookstore event.

When you reach out to local bookstores and ask to do a signing to help promote your book, bring some information on how you will be able to drive people to attend the event. Some local bookstores will have a weekly schedule of authors who rotate at a specific table. The regular customers know where to go to find the visiting author for the day. Other bookstores may have been burned by one too many poorly attended events.

If the store does not want to host an event, you can still ask them to stock your books. As a new author, you are untested and they may be hesitant to order a carton of books. If people don't buy them, the store is stuck with the inventory and may have to return the books to your distributer.

One trend that I experienced with bookstores in my local area is the option to sell books on consignment. The book store only gives up the shelf space, and then both the author and the store have an incentive to sell the book. Neither makes money until the book is sold. If your books continue to sell, the store may decide to make a larger order. At that time, they would move to a standard model where they purchase the books upfront at a wholesale discount and sell it for the list price.

Make time to frequent the events that your local book stores put on, even before your book is out. These are people who like books. Some of these stores may have regular events and book clubs that you can join as well. As an author, you need to first be a reader, so this will benefit you in many ways. Get to know the store owners. Then, when you come in to ask them to sell your book you aren't a stranger to them.

The same goes for your local libraries. Readers love the library. Your local librarians are always looking for new programming and events to bring more people out. While the library may only purchase one copy of your book, you can still get reviews from these readers or word-of-mouth promotion from library patrons.

Appeal to Book Clubs

In addition to all of the book networks that exist now, there are always age-old options too. Book clubs are an institution and still thrive in this post-internet world. Some book clubs are even exclusively digital with conversations happening online. But many are still in-person affairs with a group of people who gather at a friends' home or coffee shop to discuss a selected book.

The reason you wrote your book was likely so that readers could connect with your story or the information you wanted to share. With a book club, not only will they read the book, they will discuss it too. And they have to get a copy from somewhere. Many people I know who are in book clubs usually get their monthly books from the library because it can be expensive to buy a new book every month. If it is a popular book, they may feel the pressure to buy a copy so they can read the book by the next meeting.

One way that I market to book clubs is to have Discussion Guides for each book available online. When I can provide the questions ahead of time, I make it easier for the group leader to select my book. Not only does this person have to read the book, but they may feel put on the spot to think of questions. If they can easily download the guide, I have removed that obstacle for them.

I also aim to add value to the clubs. If I offer to attend their meeting in person or via a video-call, this can add a fun element to their discussion. I had one book club member order books for me to sign, and then she gave the signed copy to each person in the club. These little touches can help you stand apart from the other options they have to pick from.

You can easily find book clubs around you. You probably know somebody who knows somebody in a club. You can also search on Facebook or MeetUp .com for book clubs in your area or any associated with local bookstores.

It is important to know what kind of books the club reads. Some clubs may only read leadership and management books, others may stick to detective mysteries. Only market to the clubs that would want to read your book. Don't pressure a group that usually reads outside of your genre. You may end up with a dozen poor reviews on Goodreads or your retailers if the book just isn't what they like.

You have likely heard of Oprah's Book Club and the coveted "O" seal that so many authors want to see on their book cover. Reese Witherspoon and other celebrities who love to read have started book clubs as well. A recommendation by a big-name celebrity can be a huge opportunity for your book. But the odds that your book will be selected are extremely small. Instead, focus on the book clubs in your area. If you do get Oprah or Reese to add your book to their club, be sure to tell them where you learned all of your great book marketing ideas from! (Kidding – okay, not really!)

Up to this point, we have covered the basics, the fundamentals of book marketing. You have elements within your book that you can leverage to build your list and readership, you have solid reviews, and you are focused on avid readers first. Check, check, check. With these elements in place, we will look at marketing opportunities that will require more time, effort, and money to execute. From here on out, you will need to balance how much time you dedicate to marketing and how much you need to spend writing your next book.

Chapter Six

Advertising

Most of the marketing strategies I mentioned so far require your creativity and your time, but not necessarily your money. You could invest in your cover design, but you *could* create it yourself. You *could* learn the ins and outs of posting on different social channels. You have low-cost or no-cost options to promote your book.

In my career before I became a full-time author, I worked in marketing. I saw our weekly, monthly, and annual budgets for paid advertising. My eyes would bulge out of my head at the amount of money spent on pay-per-click (PPC) ads and agency fees. For this reason, I built the demand for my books without paid advertising. Especially when my books were priced at $0.99, and I was only making $0.34 per book. I didn't want to spend $0.50 or $1.00 just for someone to click to see more about my book. What if they didn't buy it? Even if they did, I would still lose money.

Before you dive into paid advertising, make sure you have done everything you can in terms of organic marketing and free promotion. You will hear authors on podcasts who talk about how they launched their books, put up some Amazon Ads, and then made 6-figures. I assure you; they are glossing over critical steps. The last thing you want to do is put yourself in a hole in terms of negative ROI (return on investment) with your ads.

I will go through the different platforms where you can advertise your book and some considerations on each.

Amazon

Amazon, initially known as an online book-seller, is now a paragon of marketing in the 21st century. *Did you mean to leave this item in your cart? Here let me email you a reminder. Did you buy a tablet? Let me tell you all about the cases and screen covers that match your exact device.* Amazon knows what you want, and they know how to sell it to you. This can be a huge benefit to you as an author. When your book does well, and Amazon is making money on it, they will promote it for you in terms of discoverability on their algorithm. At the time of this writing, this kicks-in when you have over 100 reviews for your book. To help get your book to that point, you can advertise to readers.

You may have heard these ads referred to as AMS (Amazon Marketing Services). However, Amazon has rebranded this service, and this is now the Amazon Advertising console. From here, you can create PPC (pay-per-click) campaigns to promote your books. You can target specific keywords, such as your genre, or other books or authors in your genre. For my books, I have targeted authors who wrote books in the same genre (ex. Blake Crouch), the actual books that I wanted to compare to (ex. Dark Matter), and keywords (ex. Science Fiction Multiverse).

When your ad is live, it can show up on the product results page or the lock screen on a Kindle. In my experience, when I am reading, the last thing I want to do is click on an ad. Because of this, I have focused on the sponsored product ads that show up on the results page. When a reader searches Amazon for Michael Crichton, I want my book, *The Infinite-Infinite*, to show up. I put together a campaign to target his name, a few common misspellings of his name, and a few longer keywords like "Michael Crichton Books" and "Michael Crichton Timeline." I cast a wide net to start, and then I narrow my focus as I see results come in. (NOTE: I give this example to show *how* you can target ads. Picking one of the best-selling authors on this century – or last – is not going to be as helpful. Try to pick authors and books that are comparable, but not runaway bestsellers. Everyone is trying to bid on those books.)

When you set up your ads, Amazon will show you the current range of prices per click. They will automatically give you a bid that is in the middle of that range. To start, go with what Amazon suggests. Yes, they want your money. But they want you to have successful ad campaigns so that you continue to spend money with them. It is easy to get pessimistic about a big corporation that profits off of you. But remember, Amazon only profits when you profit. Your incentives are mostly aligned. You will see clicks on your ads that will not result in any sales. This is why you need to monitor your ad performance closely so that you can optimize.

With the PPC ads, you only pay when someone clicks on your ad. You have the option to include a line or two of ad text to grab the readers' interest along with the book cover, or you can leave the ad text blank. You can modify and test the ads over time to see what gets you a better result. If you run ads and see that you have impressions (or views), but no one has clicked, then you likely need to change your ad text.

When someone clicks on your ad, they cost you money. Even if they don't buy. If you see clicks without sales, you need to look at your book's page on Amazon. Is there a quality error reported on your book? If so, fix that. Was your ad text aligned with your book description? Do you have editorial reviews to promote? You got the reader to the next step in the process. Now you need to get them to click "buy." Put yourself in the readers' shoes and look at your book critically. What would encourage your ideal reader to purchase? One way you can get an objective opinion is to ask friends to look at your ad copy.

Because you pay every time someone clicks on your ad, you may start to see that the cost can add up quickly. If you have 100 different keywords, 12 authors, and 20 books in your genre that you can target, and each is capped at $5.00 a day, you could spend hundreds of dollars in one day. This was my biggest fear when I finally decided to give Amazon Advertising a try.

I limited the number of campaigns I started with. I found a range where I would be comfortable if every campaign reached the max budget in one day. For me, that was seven campaigns. If I spent $35 in one day with no sales, I could stomach that. Over time, this number has increased as I have seen sales come in from the ads. Listen to your gut, if you feel nervous about the potential cost, cut back. If you see that an ad has received a lot of clicks, but no sales, you can pause it as you start to modify the page to increase conversions. When I started my first ads, it took me almost a week to get my first click which cost $0.41.

The important thing to remember is that there is no "set it and forget it." You should keep track of your ads daily to see how they perform. (Unless you have unlimited funds, in which case you can feel free to donate to my ad campaigns any time you like.)

As my business, and personal life, has changed so has my strategy. I realized that if I wanted to continue to dabble with Amazon Ads for my books, I needed help. In early 2022 I worked with an ads manager through Reedsy. This was a great opportunity for me to hand off one aspect of my marketing to someone who knew the system better. I could trust they knew the platform and I didn't have to keep checking in every day and optimizing. You may elect to hire someone to help as well. Be sure you understand their fees up front before you start working together.

Amazon Advertising will get you the closest to your reader and their digital shopping cart. They click on the ad and then click buy. Done. But with other advertising options, you will be one (or more) steps removed. The paid advertising options that follow will all get you one more step out. Any friction points can result in fewer sales. This means that you need to consider not only the ad you run and who you target. You need to plan for the additional steps that the reader will need to go through to purchase your book.

BookBub

There are several ways that you can advertise your book through BookBub. Daily Deals, Chirp Audiobook Deals, and Cost-Per-Click ads are all options. You can make use of any of these from the BookBub Partner Dashboard: htt ps://partners.bookbub.com/ads.

Daily Deals

The Daily Deals emails are what you will hear other authors reference when they talk about BookBub. Getting into this email can give your eBook an incredible amount of exposure. Avid readers open this email every day to find new books that they can read for free. As more readers check out your book and review it, you will grow your organic or word-of-mouth exposure. It is a long-lead strategy for you as an author.

Because of the popularity of these emails among readers, BookBub charges heavily for these placements. When I launched my first book in 2015, I looked into how I could get *Nailbiters* into this email. Other authors on the Goodreads forums shared how excited they were to be approved to be in the newsletter. I started to fill out the application myself and saw that to give my book away for free I would have to pay $700.

$700!

At the time, I charged $0.99 for my first book and made $0.34 per copy sold. I would have to sell thousands of books to make back that $700 investment. I closed out of the application as fast as I could. How could authors spend this much, just to give their books away for free? It didn't make sense to me. I'm sure the rates have gone up since then as well.

You may read this and think, "Wow, that is way too high a price!" Or you may think, "$700. That's it?" Each author will have their own tolerance for how much they want to invest in their business and how much they have available to promote their book. This is a personal decision.

For me, it did not make sense then, and it doesn't make sense now. As I look to write more books in a series, I may revisit BookBub and the Daily Deals (if my application is selected). Once I have multiple books in one series, it may make financial sense to give the first away for free to drive more people into the series. If they get book #1 for free, but pay for books #2 and #3, then I can earn back the cost.

Audio Deals

BookBub started to offer similar promotions for audiobooks. BookBub also owns the audiobook retail platform, Chirp. They send similar newsletters with new releases and featured audiobook deals to their audience each day. Authors who have audiobooks available through Chirp.com can apply on the BookBub Partners Platform to have their book featured. When these deals were first offered it was at no cost to the author. (WOW!) However, they have recently changed the format so that the author pays 10% of the sales generated from the promotion. So, if the promotion doesn't move any audiobooks, the author pays nothing for the placement. If it helps to sell thousands, then BookBub gets a portion.

If your audiobook is selected, you have to go in to Findaway Voices (INAudio) to update the price discount for the promotional period. Findaway Voices makes it easy for authors to do this on their platform.

Cost Per Click/ Pay Per Click Ads

The third way to do paid ads via BookBub is their cost-per-click (CPC) or pay-per-click ads (PPC). Similar to how Amazon Advertising works, you can select the genre or similar authors you want your book ad to show next to. The targeting is not as exact or precise as Amazon, however on BookBub you are advertising to book lovers, you already know that whoever sees your ad is looking for something to read.

As with other CPC ads, you only pay when someone clicks the link. But where will the link send them? When you set your campaign you can set the links for Amazon, Barnes & Noble, Apple, and other vendors that carry your books. The reader's preferred vendor will display when they click on your ad.

You can test the ad text and creative to optimize for more clicks. The campaign set up process allows you to make an ad with your book cover image or you can upload your own 300x250 pixel ad.

I tried these ads for a bit. They didn't spend anywhere near the budget that I set. But I couldn't see if any of my clicks resulted in sales. Sure, I had sales during the same time period the ads were running, but I couldn't say for certain if they were from the ads or just people finding my books through my YouTube channel or podcast interviews.

Facebook

Facebook is a big online gathering place. If your book is about permaculture and sustainability, you can find people who are interested in that topic and advertise to them. If your book is about personal finance, you can target that group as well. In addition to targeting Facebook users based on any books they like; you can target based on any number of interests and demographics. For example, my fourth book, *The Infinite-Infinite* is about the multiverse and time-travel. I can target people who liked the TV show Timeless and who also like to read because I think they will enjoy the book. The point here is that you have a lot of options. You might even say that you have too many options. The more you refine your audience, the more expensive your ads will be, generally speaking.

You can do a text ad with an image, or a video ad, or an ad with multiple images that highlight all the books in your series. You will probably get dizzy with ideas for ads. Keep an ongoing list of ideas for what you would like to try. Start small with a sample budget to get the hang of the system before you go big.

There are many caveats and strategies for optimizing Facebook advertising. Some say you should create a video and promote it with a paid ad. Then put everyone who watched the video in a new ad group and target them with a new ad to get them to your book's page or an email subscription page. There are an infinite number of strategies you can choose from.

Similar to Amazon Advertising, you can set a daily maximum on your advertising spend for each click. However, with Amazon, you may find that you often don't hit the daily cap. That will likely not be the case with Facebook. If you say that you want to spend up to $5 a day, there is a very high chance that you will spend all $5 in one day.

If you decide to run Facebook ads, have them come from your Facebook Author's page. Even if those who view the ad don't take your desired action and click through to purchase the book or join your email list, they can still click on your account profile and see what you are offering there. If they are curious, you want to give them every option to connect with you.

One thing to keep in mind, Facebook doesn't like it when you link outside of Facebook. After allegations of data breaches and potential interference by outside parties in the 2016 election with "fake news" against both major candidates, Facebook updated their algorithm to put any post that links outside of Facebook way down in the rankings. Whether you believe in the election interference is none of my business, but the changes that Facebook made impacts everyone. If you want to do a Facebook post about your book and provide a link to the Barnes & Noble page where someone can buy it, chances are your followers and friends won't see it. Unless you "boost" the post. This is a one-time paid ad to promote a single post that you have already posted as opposed to a campaign that will run to people you specifically target. You can update the targeting on your boosted post as well.

After a few ad campaigns or post boosts, you will start to see what people respond to. Maybe they are more comfortable with a post that directs them to Goodreads so they can add the book to their reading list. This type of ad doesn't ask them to part with their information or any money. Or maybe people just want to get to the point and make the purchase. Your audience will show you what they want based on the content they do and do not interact with.

One way that you can save when you get started with Facebook ads is to take advantage of the credits that they offer. Every so often you will see a notification that one of your organic posts is doing well and that if you boost the post it will reach more people. Facebook will include a $5 credit sometimes to sweeten the deal. Take it! It's free advertising money for you to play with. They want you to try it out, have a successful campaign, and then pay full price for your next ad.

You can also elect to test the waters to understand it yourself and then reinvest your royalties to pay someone to run these ads for you. Just as with any other advertising, these campaigns should be closely monitored and optimized. It can help you to hire a professional who is up to date on all of the algorithm changes and has worked on countless campaigns. Some will ask to be paid a flat rate for their services or they may ask to receive a commission on the sales you receive from the ad.

Google

I heard someone once say that if you don't pay for a service, you are the commodity. Most people understand that with Google, we can search for free, maintain email accounts at no charge, and watch countless hours of cat videos on YouTube because we are the commodity. Our attention is the product. Google places ads in each part of its ecosystem. In general, people don't mind this because of the value they receive and have learned how to spot an ad versus an organic result. Some people don't like this and won't use Google at all. But we will focus on most people, and your readers are likely using Google.

Because I saw first-hand the expensive cost of Google PPC ads in my professional career, I have avoided them for my books. Google Ads can be effective, but many components go into each ad. You have to understand what readers search for on Google. If someone searches for "great science fiction book to read," I could bid on that exact search (a long tail phrase match keyword) and try to be the very top result. Or I could go for a broader branding approach and target "self-publishing tips for first-time authors." I could also try to build my brand as an author and show up for "authors in Florida" if I think that a news show or podcast might want to interview someone like me.

Try to rank **organically** first, before you spend a lot of time and money on paid Google ads. This type of advertising might work best for your local bookstore so that they show up when someone searches for "bookstore near me." But, as an author, you have limited time and funds. Until you sell a lot of books, then you can hire someone to run your SEO and SEM campaigns.

Book Newsletters

Up until now, I've mentioned the big advertising options. Options with a large reach and the potential to be very expensive. With cost-per-click ads, regardless of the platform, you have the potential to spend a lot of money with one campaign. Each platform allows you to set a maximum budget. But what if you spend all of it in one day, before you even get to optimize the ads?

Book newsletters offer a more targeted approach – the audience already likes to read. You pick which newsletter to be in, likely one based on genre.

Authors usually pick a genre specific newsletter, a date, and send in the details about their book. The cost is fixed. No surprises or maxing out on budget too early.

Written Word Media hosts newsletters based on genre (ex. Romance) or price (ex. Free Booksy and Bargain Booksy). The Fussy Librarian hosts multiple newsletters by genre as well as retailer. The newsletters usually prefer to promote books that are on sale or permanently discounted. You can advertise a new book or an older one, depending on the newsletter focus. This gives subscribers a reason to open the newsletter and buy now.

For new authors starting out, this may be one of the more cost-effective options. The paid services I mentioned here are a start and not the entire spectrum of paid advertising available to you as an author. There are companies you can pay to organize a book tour for you on different blogs and podcasts. There are ads that you can run on any number of websites. Because you are marketing your first book, you want to stay broad and look at the widest opportunities before you narrow down on your strategy. If you feel that you don't have the budget to do any paid advertising for your first book, that is fine too. I didn't start paid advertising for a year after my first book was released. It may have kept my sales slow, but it was what I was comfortable with. Keep a written note with your royalty per book and what advertising budget you are comfortable with. Reference this paper when paid advertising opportunities arise. If the deal sounds great, but it is way above your budget, say no. Don't jump on the new shiny opportunity because they had great promotional copy or you feel that your book sales have hit a slump. Each advertising campaign should be strategic, not reactionary. This written note will be a reminder that you have made a plan and you will only revise it if and when you are ready to make a larger strategic change.

Chapter Seven

Continuous Marketing Efforts

I t can feel overwhelming to try and get all of your marketing dialed in for the exact date that your book launches. You want to put your best foot forward to help with your sales, but you are just one person. As a self-published author, you will wear many hats and it is okay if you need to take one or two off from time-to-time. While maximizing your sales rankings and reviews in the first thirty days that your book is live is critical, your books aren't going anywhere. You will be able to continually promote your book for years. Don't lose sight of the long-term marketing tactics that are just as effective and can keep you from pulling out your hair trying to synchronize everything.

Podcast Appearances

Clients have asked me when they should pitch podcasts to interview them about their book. Here are a few of my key considerations when it comes to podcast guesting for authors.

Podcasts exist to entertain and inform. They do not exist to promote your book. When you pitch a podcast, you need to first show that you can provide the audience with valuable and actionable information. Tailor your pitch to specifically fit what the podcast host is looking for. When you are interviewed, be sure that you provide actionable information to the audience. One critical tip that I know applies to all authors, regardless of genre: do NOT send your manuscript along with your pitch. In general, don't ever send anyone an unsolicited manuscript of your book. If they want to read it, they'll ask for a copy.

The only bad time to be on a podcast is when you don't have a way for people to take action on your information. It is okay to schedule a podcast interview before your book is on pre-order if you can direct the audience to a lead generation form. It is better if you can direct them to the pre-order page. It is best if you can direct them to a live listing. Podcast interviews are listened to the day that they are released, but many listeners will catch up on old episodes weeks, months, or years later.

For those who regularly listen to podcasts, you may notice that when a big-name author launches a book, they seem to be on every podcast that you listen to. This is an effective strategy to be on a major podcast the week your book releases. But if you say the same thing over and over and that is all a listener hears from you that week, they may decide not to buy. You need to find a fine balance and get the word out to as wide an audience as possible. When you repeat the same piece of advice on every podcast, it starts to sound like that's all you have to say, so why would they buy your book?

Instead, focus on a few podcasts to coincide with your book release, but try to spread out your other interviews both before and after the book launches.

You may think that people will only want to talk with you when your book is released. My third book, *Enemies of Peace*, was published in November 2017. I still did interviews for that book over two years later.

Automate Where You Can

As an author, you will have a lot to do. If you are juggling a family, a day-job, and time with friends in addition to your writing, you will need to find a way to automate where you can. The question to ask yourself when you are doing a tedious task is, "can I automate this?" Sometimes the answer will be no, but it could also be yes.

There are many automation tools available today that any entrepreneur can make use of. The key thing is to make sure that you don't spend all of your limited time creating new automations to the point that you have a new complex web to manage. These tools and systems should make life easier, not the other way around.

My first tip when it comes to automating is don't automate what you don't understand. Don't start with a new channel and automate right away. Go through the process manually a few times. This will help you to understand how things should work. It will also help you to understand where the automation might break. I use limited automation in my business, but the few that I do use are simple one-step processes that I can easily troubleshoot when I need to.

One of the biggest things to remember about marketing in the 21st century is that you need to make a connection with your reader. When they feel like they can post something on social media and you will respond, that builds the connection. They have a reason to root for you.

DO NOT AUTOMATE THIS. I have seen bloggers and writers try to automate these kinds of "authentic" messages. People are smart and will figure out that there is nothing authentic about this. Instead of creating a positive connection, you will leave the reader feeling as though they are just another number. Don't set an auto-response tweet for anytime someone mentions you or follows you. Don't try to be clever with an automated response to everyone who tags you on Instagram. Don't automate your authenticity.

Optimize Your Book Descriptions

Your book description is marketing copy. The chance that you crafted the exact perfect book description on the first try is very small.

I have seen some authors post different options on Facebook groups for authors and go with whatever the group selected. I've seen the same on Goodreads groups as well. This can work. But if those authors aren't your target audience, you may still need to test these options live.

Put your best book description into your publishing platforms for your pre-sale and launch. Set a calendar reminder to change the copy out every 90 days. Some experts say to change it out every month. What if you change out your copy on December 1st and see amazing sales for that month compared to previous months? You might think that you've found a winner. Or maybe, that is the biggest month for retail sales all year. By looking at these trends every quarter, you get a better feel for whether one book description works over another in the long run.

Also, you're an author and have approximately a million things to do for your business. Set realistic timelines for these optimizations.

"More Books Sell More Books"

One of my good friends, who also happens to be an author, repeated this phrase to me once. I don't know the exact origins, but it seems to be widely accepted among most authors. It is the answer to the greatest question that every author has: how can I sell more copies of my book?

"More books sell more books."

You may find that you only have one book in you. Your story has been told, and you can rest now. In that case, you will have a lot of time to focus on the marketing minutiae. But for everyone else, for those who dream of making a career of their writing, this is the simplest answer.

Should I focus on having an appearance at a book fair every weekend for the next year or write my next book?

Should I spend the money on this blog tour for my current book or write my next book?

Should I learn how to do Facebook ads or write my next book?

If you have the time, money, and energy to do all those things - go for it. But if you have a finite supply of all three, focus on your next book. Of course, you need a readership and a steady following to sell that next book, but no one can buy it if you don't write it.

Your marketing will never be "done." There will never be a time where you can cross this off of your to-do list. There are always new readers out there who have yet to discover your book. Find a system that works for you and that you can sustain over time.

Chapter Eight
Building a Readership

R emember, you are just starting out. It is easy to look at other authors that you admire and wish you had their fan base and publicity. Everyone started where you are right now. Be thoughtful about your marketing, and observe what does and doesn't seem to move the needle for your books. Yes, you want to sell more books, but you want to get them in front of the right audience. Selling 1,000 copies to those who will never read it will create a short-term spike in your sales, that's it. Selling 1,000 copies of your book to the right readers can make a big impact on your ability to continue to write and sell more books.

It Takes Time

"At the speed of light? The speed of sound? The speed of literature?"
Escaping Avila Chase, M.K. Williams

Books take a long time. To write them, to edit them, and for most consumers, to read them. Give yourself a reasonable timeframe to build a readership. And I don't mean a month or a year. It can take multiple years to build up your readership. It takes time for people to discover and then read your book. Don't give up too early, before you've had a chance to let your book get into the market.

You may be working to market your first book, but chances are it won't be your last. Know that the longevity of your career as an author is the true measure of success, not the instant gratification of one month of top sales followed by years of minuscule numbers.

Capture Interest on Your Terms

As I mentioned earlier, having a method to capture email addresses will be a long-term strategy for your success. There are spam compliance laws you will need to adhere to for specific states and countries. But, if Facebook shuts down or Goodreads changes their functionality, or any other unforeseeable disruption occurs on your author platform, the list of interested readers that you can communicate with through email will aid in your long-term success.

I spent my workdays optimizing email campaigns and lead forms. I had to be up on the latest compliance laws, so I saw red-tape everywhere when it came to email marketing. The last thing I wanted to do was bring my day-job into my sacred writing and book marketing time. I'm paying the price now for stubbornly refusing to capture email consent sooner. My list is woefully small compared to other authors who started their business at the same time as me. Learn from my mistake: it is never too soon to start building your email list.

Most email service providers (ESPs) for small businesses come with built-in compliance and opt-in functionality. They also usually offer a free option of their service to users who have lists smaller than 1,000-2,000 subscribers. This can be a great way to start to curate your list, but be sure to read up on email compliance as well. These laws tend to change often, so do a quick search for "Email Compliance + COUNTRY/STATE" to see the biggest items that you need to consider for your audience.

Connect with Readers

Yes, you want these readers to buy your book, leave a rave review, and anxiously wait by their devices for a notification that your next book is out. But remember, your readers are people too. They're not just machines that will purchase your book on command. Don't make all of your marketing about, "buy my book, buy my book, buy my book!" Post about your inspiration, your distractions, and your progress on the book as you write it. Share the books that you are reading and enjoying. Endorse other authors who your readers might enjoy while they wait for your next book. A person will read more than one book in their life, your competition isn't with other authors. Your competition is the distractions that will keep you from getting your next book finished.

Find a system that works for you to authentically connect with readers. If you are already on Twitter a lot, be responsive on that channel. When people ask how they can connect with you, let them know that is your preferred medium. It may take you a few tries to find what fits and that may evolve. Be open about that. And when you need to take a hiatus from social media to work on your next book, just put up that post and let your readers know that you'll be back once you write that manuscript. The excitement will build as they anticipate your return.

Chapter Nine

Conclusion

After going through this book, your marketing to-do list should be full. Don't worry, there will be time to take care of each item. With all of the different things that we could do, or feel that we *should* do, to market our books, it is a wonder that we ever have time to write another one.

What I want you to take away from this book is that there are so many possible options for you to explore as you promote your book. Each avenue has its pros and cons, each has a different cost, and each will have a different outcome based on your book and your unique audience.

There is no magic pill that will solve all of your book marketing needs. Sorry, it just doesn't work that way.

Now that you are aware of each of these options, I want you to take a moment to write out the three things that you can do each week (or month if that is all your schedule allows) to help promote your books. If you have a full-time day job and a family in addition to your books, those three things may be difficult to fit in. I am a full-time author, and I can still find so many things to do instead of marketing. There will always be other things that we can do instead, but if we stick to these three things, we will make progress. As time goes on those three things may change, or you may be able to add on more.

But for starters, pick three things. Before I left my day job, these were my three tasks:

1. Anytime someone added one of my books on Goodreads or left a

review I would "like" it and leave a "thank you" comment.

2. One post a week on my Author's Facebook page showing a lifestyle-based photo with one of my books strategically placed in the shot.

3. Post about the next book I was working on.

Those are all simple and small. I wasn't selling thousands of copies a week by doing this, far from it. But I was moving forward every day.

Here are some other tasks that you can try to incorporate into your week:

- Send a guest request to a podcast in your genre

- Create alternative descriptions for your book

- Take photos of your book to post at a later time

- Curate a playlist for your work in progress and post it to your platform

- Add a blog post to your author website

What will your go-forward strategy be for promoting your book? My answer is a question back to you. What are the elements that I outlined in this book that resonated with you? Focus on the easy to execute tasks first and then work your way up to the more complex items.

Best of luck as you promote your book and get it in front of new readers who will love your story!

Bibliography

Perrin, Andrew. "One-in-five Americans nowlisten to audiobooks." Pew Research Center. September 25, 2019. https://www.pewresearch.org/fact-tank/2019/09/25/one-in-five-americans-now-listen-to-audiobooks/.

Amazon Community Guidelines. "Customer Reviews" https://www.amazon.com/gp/help/customer/display.html?nodeId=201967050

Chesson, Dave. "How to Create a Professional AuthorPage in Amazon Author Central." KindlepreneurPodcast. https://kindlepreneur.com/amazon-author-central-page/

Resources

More questions? Schedule some time to connect with me directly or check out my YouTube Channel.

Books2Read:
https://books2read.com/links/ubl/create/

Facebook Groups:
IngramSpark Author Community
https://www.facebook.com/groups/641752356577267
Wide for the Win:
https://www.facebook.com/groups/556186621558858

YouTube Channels:
M.K. Williams: https://youtube.com/mkwilliamsauthor
Keith Wheeler Books: https://www.youtube.com/c/keithwheelerbooks

Podcasts:
The Creative Penn with Joanna Penn: https://podcasts.apple.com/gb/podcast/the-creative-penn-podcast-for-writers/id309426367
Alliance of Independent Authors: https://podcasts.apple.com/us/podcast/askalli-self-publishing-advice-podcast/id1080135033?mt=2

The Indy Author: https://www.theindyauthor.com/podcast.html

Podcasting for Authors: https://www.theindyauthor.com/podcasting-for -authors.html

Services:

Grammarly: https://grammarly.go2cloud.org/SH2QA

100 Covers: http://100covers.com/?ref=49

BookBrush https://bookbrush.com/

Advertising Platforms for Authors:

Amazon Advertising: https://advertising.amazon.com/

BookBub: https://partners.bookbub.com/ads

Author Bio

M.K. Williams is an author and independent publisher. She left her career in sports marketing to pursue writing and publishing full-time in 2019. She has published three novels, one financial workbook, and a collection of short stories. In addition to publishing her own works, she has helped established companies bring their information to the masses through publishing books under their own brands. She focuses on helping aspiring authors realize their dreams. When she isn't writing she enjoys running and reading in her spare time.

Thank you so much for reading: *Book Marketing for the First-Time Author*. I hope that you enjoyed reading it as much as I enjoyed writing it.

If you found this book helpful, please take a moment to leave a review. This helps other first-time authors find this book to help them on their journey.

You can download your Marketing Priority Checklist at AuthorYourAmbition.com/Marketing-Priority-Checklist.

I would love to hear from you as you continue to market your books to hear what has worked for you and how you have put this information to use. You can reach me at authoryourambition@gmail.com.

WHAT IS YOUR NEXT READ?

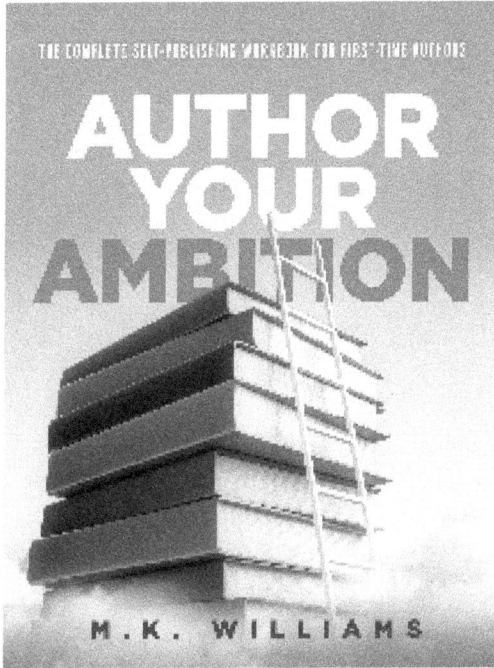

Author Your Ambition: The Complete Self-Publishing Workbook for First-Time Authors